Praise for *Sly & the Family Stone*

"Joel Selvin, the veteran music critic of the *San Francisco Chronicle*, published a thoroughgoing, book-length oral history of the group in 1998 (simply called *Sly & the Family Stone: An Oral History*) that is as disturbing and chilling a version as you'll ever find of the 'dashed '60s dream' narrative: idealism giving way to disillusionment, soft drugs giving way to hard, ferment to rot.

It's agreed upon by everyone Selvin interviewed—which is pretty much everyone in Stone's family, band, and circle of hangers-on, apart from Sly himself—that the bad craziness began when he forsook the Bay Area for Southern California, in 1970. Exit the music of hope and the gorgeous mosaic; enter firearms, coke, PCP, goons, paranoia, isolation, and a mean-spirited pet pit bull named Gun."

—**David Kamp**, "Sly Stone's Higher Power" *Vanity Fair*, August 2007

SLY & THE FAMILY STONE

AN ORAL HISTORY

JOEL SELVIN

PERMUTED
PRESS

A PERMUTED PRESS BOOK
ISBN: 978-1-63758-502-3
ISBN (eBook): 978-1-63758-503-0

Sly & the Family Stone:
An Oral History
© 1998 by Joel Selvin
All Rights Reserved

Cover art by Tiffani Shea

Permuted Press, LLC
New York • Nashville
permutedpress.com

Published in the United States of America
1 2 3 4 5 6 7 8 9 10

FOR HAMP DA BUBBA DA BANKS
You made this book what it is.

Contents

Notes on the Second Edition.. ix
Introduction to the First Edition xiii
The Voices... xxiii

ONE: A Little Prince 1
TWO: Really a Rhythm and Blues Cat 22
THREE: Boys, Girls, Black, White 35
FOUR: Pussycat a Go-Go, The Electric Circus 48
FIVE: Playing Toilets... 59
SIX: As Big As Life... 82
SEVEN: The Riot Was Already Going On 98
EIGHT: Guns and Dogs 116
NINE: Sly's Last Chance 139
TEN: Time to Go 151
ELEVEN: Only Kidding.. 170
TWELVE: Nobody Believed Anymore 194

Thank You 211
Discography 213
Photo Credits 219
About the Author.. 221

NOTES ON THE SECOND EDITION

Sly Stone: The Oral History was originally commissioned as part of a series, "Off the Record," edited by esteemed music journalist Dave Marsh, who intended to shine lights on forgotten corners of music history. At the time, Sly had only recently re-emerged from years as a fugitive from justice, his reputation shredded, his stature in the music world at an all-time low. The band members and their associates had seen the group's legacy almost disappear and when I set out to collect their stories, they were scattered far and wide, all long separated from the world of Sly Stone, and, almost to a man or woman, anxious to tell their stories.

Freddie Stewart, Sly's hapless younger brother, was leading a congregation at a ramshackle church in Vallejo, not far from where he'd grown up, but driving a school bus for disabled children for a living. Cynthia Robinson was practically homeless, sleeping on her daughter's floor in Sacramento and making sandwiches at lunch rush for a local delicatessen. Jerry Martini was living in Honolulu and playing sax nightly in a hotel lounge. Larry Graham was staying in a Jehovah's Witness compound in Jamaica and doing Sly's act with his band, which included Sister Rose on vocals. Rose Stewart was cordial and welcoming when we first met, gladly agreeing to speak, until she learned I had been talking to her ex-husband, Hamp. That stopped her cold. She left me sitting in a San Fernando Valley restaurant for forty-five minutes before phoning the manager to say she wasn't coming. David Kapralik met me at his home in Haiku and treated me immediately like an old friend. "I knew you were coming," he said that first night in Maui. "Of course, not you specifically…" We remained close for the rest of his life.

Nobody had ever asked Hamp Banks about his time in the midst of Sly & the Family Stone and simply finding him was an enterprise. Hamp had spent his life living outside the law and there were few official records associated with him other than a 1964 marriage that had ended long before. After all the regulation methods of locating interview subjects failed to turn up any information on the public record, I set out on foot to check hair salons in Hunters Point, where Hamp had last been sighted. At the first shop, they knew about him and directed me to a lonely ghetto barber shop on Third Street behind a set of Venetian blinds, where my inquiry was met with grave suspicion. The gentleman in the barber's chair having his haircut spoke. "We haven't seen Hamp in a while," he said. I left my card.

Two nights later, I answered the phone and a deep, resonant, soon-to-be familiar voice said "I found you." He came over the next night and sat in my office ready to tell his story for the first time. He glanced at a compact disc on my desk, an English reissue of some early Sly Stone recordings including a number of unreleased masters. "'Every Dog Has Its Day' was one of my favorites," he said, citing a little known Sly Stone song from before his days with the group. And then he began singing the lyrics.

Like he always did, Hamp dived into the project, not only sitting for hours of astonishing interviews, but calling the other gangsters and getting them to participate. He became something of an executive producer of the book. His involvement had a surprising effect on the members of the band, who hadn't seen him in years but, in many cases, remained wary and intimidated by Hamp.

Like many survivors of catastrophic trauma, the members of Sly & the Family Stone had adopted a storyline that hid the truth and protected the guilty. The horrors and abuse they went through left scorch marks that time had not erased, but they had managed to stay true to a sunny, optimistic narrative, avoiding the most horrific details in their retellings. After Hamp had painted a more authentic picture—with fine-point detail—subsequent interviews with band members took a different tone. "One thing about Hamp," admitted drummer Gregg Errico, "he's no bullshitter."

Hamp got Bobby Womack to finally return my calls. He introduced me to James "J.B." Brown in Salt Lake City. He phoned me in Los Angeles, where I was attending a concert, and sent me to meet Eddie Chin at his Hollywood Chocolate Potato Chip Factory. "Who's Eddie Chin?" I asked. "He'll tell you," Hamp said.

Hamp and I would have many escapades after the Sly book. Our friendship bloomed over the telling of the story. He wrote punctuation-free, uncapitalized emails that he invariably signed "yr friend for life." I spoke at his funeral, along with Freddie Stewart from the group and San Francisco Mayor London Breed. He was always so proud of his contributions to this book, which is now properly dedicated to him and his memory.

These people, for the most part, had never before been approached to offer comprehensive accounts of their time in the extraordinary scene in which they found themselves and they poured out their experiences willingly. These were not necessarily fond memories. Everybody had moved on many years before, but they recalled their time in the Sly & the Family Stone world in vivid, intense, and exhausting sessions. They would not ever be so willing again.

Over the years, this slim volume has become a kind of Rosetta Stone for Sly Stone scholars, a minor classic in the field. I have provided copies of the tape transcripts to many researchers who have used the material in books, magazine articles, and films. I myself wrote a cover story for *Mojo* magazine in August 2001 about the making of *There's a Riot Goin' On* based on the transcripts. In his 2007 *Vanity Fair* profile of Sly Stone on the occasion of one his pathetic comeback attempts, David Kamp cited the book as "as disturbing and chilling a version as you'll ever find of the 'dashed '60s dream' narrative."

The music made by the original version of Sly & the Family Stone will live forever. It became the basis for an entire school of music called funk. It changed the historic direction of jazz in the hands of Miles Davis and Herbie Hancock. It perfectly symbolized the aspirations of the Woodstock generation in anthems like "I Want to Take You Higher" and others. The band made a mark that will never disappear. As the full account of their journey, this book, I humbly submit, will stand.

—Joel Selvin, March 2022

INTRODUCTION TO
THE FIRST EDITION

"Sly Stone was important," said the saxophonist. "Like Duke Ellington." His name doesn't matter, wouldn't ring any bells, but as a journeyman musician who has plowed the fuzzy boundaries of funk and jazz for a living over the past four decades, he speaks with the authority of someone who knows. There was Black music before Sly Stone and there was Black music after Sly Stone. Simple as that.

Sly Stone showed Miles Davis what to do as much as he rewrote the book of love for Motown, which were the polar extremities of contemporary Black music at the time. Stories are told about Berry Gordy Jr. brandishing copies of *Stand!* at Motown music staff meetings and Herbie Hancock imagining a new future for contemporary jazz on first hearing Sly. His magnificence may be less frequently recalled today. But Sly Stone, as the man said, was important.

He transformed the first-generation soul of Ray Charles and James Brown into a new sound that came to be called funk. He liberated artists as diverse as Miles Davis and Stevie Wonder. He created large parts of the musical visions so deftly appropriated by the likes of Parliament-Funkadelic, Michael Jackson, and Prince. He revoked how harmony vocals sounded in Black music much the same way Brian Wilson did in White pop. The deeply ingrained imprint he left on music survives, even as the man and his music continue to fade into the mists of history.

But as monumental as the music was, the story behind the songs and the man himself are nothing short of an epic American tale, largely untold until now. Many of the people interviewed for this book have never spoken about their experiences before and many of the others have never publicly discussed some of these matters. It is easy to understand their reluctance.

The young Black rock and roller who fused Black and White music was born Sylvester Stewart on March 15, 1941, in Denton, Texas, but grew up in Vallejo, California. A good kid who pretended he was bad, he presided over his own downfall with the mad glee of a child playing with matches. He turned his back on the church that raised him and summoned the very fires of perdition. His manager once recognized in Sly the timeless image of Icarus, the man who flew too close to the sun, as the fire that burned within raged out of control.

The same manager, David Kapralik, also discussed the dichotomy he saw between Sly Stone and Sylvester Stewart with a writer for *Rolling Stone*. This distinction worked its way into the entire Sly Stone mythos—although Sly/Syl himself took pains to deny it in the very next edition of the magazine. Even his father and mother have used the phraseology. It is an oversimplification to write off Sly's internal tempest to a dualistic character. But clearly he was a man in deep conflict with himself, somebody who felt the strain of pretending to be something he wasn't, and someone who took advantage of his enormous popular acceptance to indulge in some recklessly irresponsible, often evil, private program.

At the time, it was Sly who first came to symbolize the Woodstock era—his face on the movie poster, his songs on the soundtrack, his preachy parameters laid out in songs he sang that night before Woodstock's fabled half-million like "You Can Make It If You Try," "I Want To Take You Higher," "Sing a Simple Song," and, of course, "Everyday People." With an astute reading of the cultural climate, Sly Stone sketched the agenda of the Woodstock generation. His glitzy group boasted men and women, Black and White, putting into practice the left-wing principles of his songs. And the seeds for his "different strokes for different folks" sermonizing can easily be found in his own life experience.

Growing up in blue-collar, racially mixed Vallejo—about forty minutes north of San Francisco, but a thousand miles away—Sly was not a street kid. His family stayed close to the church, but young Sylvester developed a lifelong infatuation with the ghetto street mentality from afar.

His Utopian view of the races could have come from his first brush with success in the music business—a Vallejo-based doo-wop group called The Viscaynes, whose near-miss, "Yellow Moon," earned some airplay on local radio and landed Sly on local TV shows before he left high school. He was the only Black in the group and was allegedly sleeping with one of the group's two females. Of course, Sly often had beautiful White girlfriends; famed San Francisco topless dancer Carol Doda was another early one.

His first success in the record business was a rock and roll hit, "C'mon and Swim," by Black rocker Bobby Freeman, whose 1958 smash, "Do You Wanna Dance," made him San Francisco's first rock and roll star. At age nineteen, young Sly—under the sponsorship of local teen kingpins Tom Donahue and Bobby Mitchell—wrote, produced, and played on this, his first gold record. With the royalties, he moved his family out of Vallejo into a big house on the outskirts of San Francisco. His father quit his janitor business.

His next successes were all White rock and roll records—writing and producing chart singles with English-sounding rock groups like the Beau Brummels, Mojo Men, the Vejtables, the Chosen Few, and others for Donahue and Mitchell's label, Autumn Records. He apparently threw up his hands attempting to regulate the untamed, undisciplined energy of the city's nascent acid rock groups—but not before conducting demo sessions with The Charlatans and the Warlocks (before the latter changed their name to Grateful Dead). He also recorded the original version of "Somebody to Love," by the Great Society, a group featuring on vocals the young Grace Slick, who soon took the song and joined the Jefferson Airplane.

By that time, Sly was already popping as a swinging young disc jockey, jive-spieling between records on the upstart KSOL, his incandescent character lighting up the Bay Area radio dial nightly and driving the rebel soul station up in the ratings. He fashioned Sly and the Family Stone—a group that, like The Viscaynes, featured male and female members, Blacks and whites—while he reigned supreme among Bay Area soul deejays. He was already a figure to be reckoned with, showing up in an elegant Edwardian suit to an obligatory radio station promotion appearance introducing a James Brown concert in San Francisco or tooling around town in a Jaguar XKE he had painted purple. He could also already be found after his radio shift singing "In the Midnight Hour" and other soul hits in front of a routine, if not indifferent, ghetto soul band in a small club on the fringes of San Francisco's Mission District.

But right from the start, his new group was something different. He moved the scene of the crime to the suburbs down the peninsula.

At teen hot spots catering to the car crowd like Winchester Cathedral and Wayne Manor—far removed from the city's psychedelic ballrooms, in places where people still lived like Archie comic books—Sly and the Family Stone attracted a largely White audience. But given that the group's creator counted chief among his artistic reference points Bob Dylan, The Beatles, and beatnik hip-ster monologist Lord Buckley, he was already far from the everyday soul band leader.

With David Kapralik, an older, more sophisticated, Jewish record business executive from New York, Sly found a co-conspir-ator who brought even more diversity to the mix as manager. The first album, *A Whole New Thing* (1967), announced his intentions. Witty, twinkly eyed, and hip, the album reflected its maker but fell on deaf ears. The subsequent retrenchment, *Dance to the Music* (1968), found Sly pulling out all the stops.

This time there would be no ignoring him.

By the time he unleashed "Everyday People," that perfect pop single bursting with crafty sloganeering and the easy platitudes so attuned to the sensibilities of the day, he had honed both his music and ideology to laser-sharp precision. But equality of the races is today no longer a burning issue in the pop landscape of post-affir-mative action America. With the theme running through his entire career abandoned by a society that probably never needed its mes-sage more, Sly's music continues to drift off into oldies-but-good-ies land, unappreciated in a world that exalts his puerile imitators and pantywaist pretenders.

Had Sly Stone been White, would he be as lionized today as rock musicians with whom his name was once spoken in a sin-gle breath—John Lennon, Jim Morrison, Bob Dylan? Despite his oh-so-public dissipation and fall from grace, he does not even offer up a convenient corpse over which to lay hosannas. But time does not diminish his greatest work.

The twin peaks of his career—*Stand!* (1969) and *There's a Riot Goin' On* (1971)—are flip sides of the same coin. While the bril-liant *Stand!* is an extroverted, cynical pop record, *Riot* finds a now-you-see-him-now-you-don't Sly Stone sorting through his psychic detritus in a disturbing masterpiece, as deeply personal an artistic event as Brian Wilson's *Pet Sounds*, Bob Dylan's *Blonde On Blonde*, or John Lennon's *Imagine*.

Stand! was the culmination of four consecutive albums by the original group—Sly Stone (keyboards, guitar, vocals); Freddie Stone (guitar, vocals); Rose Stone (keyboards, vocals); Larry Graham (bass, vocals); Cynthia Robinson (trumpet, vocals); Jerry Martini (saxophone); Gregg Errico (drums)—with Sly acting as songwriter and record producer. Each subsequent release shows a more polished version of the emerging signature style of Sly Stone—the loopy beats, the offbeat vocalizations, the witty, pungent lyrics. Racial lines dissolved in front of him. *Stand!* achieves a seamless blend of rock and soul—but then it comes from the former boy wonder record producer with the Beatles haircut who made all those Beau Brummels and Mojo Men records.

Stand! was perfectly poised at the intersection of several musical, social, and political crossroads and glistened with a command of studio technology uncommon at the time. The record is, by turns, flagrantly transparent ("Everyday People"), openly manipulative ("I Want to Take You Higher"), and a cynical self-justification ("Sing a Simple Song") and still manages to maintain a jaunty, almost cocky swagger, underscored by deft wordsmanship born of Sly's scrupulous study of the works of Dylan.

In the two-year gap that separated *Stand!* and *Riot*, Sly managed one measly single release—the sweeping "Thank You (Falettinme Be Mice Elf Agin)," backed with "Everybody Is a Star," a creative crescendo that offered a definitive two-pronged statement from Sly responding to his popular acceptance.

The less readily understood *Riot* finds Sly offering glimpses inside his troubled heart. Or does he? He is the man in the mirror, recording spare, drab, even deadened tonalities and dry, unprocessed vocals that create an illusion of heightened intimacy. His character remains elusive, but his spirit is all over this record—whimsical, charming, sarcastic, evil, arrogant, truthful. It is a record of immense desperation and despair recorded under dire circumstances.

Nobody seems to know exactly who is playing on *There's a Riot Goin' On*. Drummer Gregg Errico, who had supposedly left the group by then, hears himself on one track. But then Larry Graham, who left the group well before *Fresh* (1973) was recorded, hears himself on that album.

While the observers all agree that *Fresh* is largely Sly playing by himself, everyone remembers the *Riot* sessions as marathon free-for-alls where he presided over a spirit of communal creativity. Bobby Womack and Billy Preston are among the acknowledged musicians who appear on the album, and other figures like Miles Davis, Ike Turner, Johnny "Guitar" Watson, and Herbie Hancock, alongside unknowns like Joe Hicks and Jimmy Ford, were also around when sessions were held.

Even though *Fresh* finds Sly slipping into second-rate work, the album's high points would fuel a dozen lesser careers. He pushed the boundaries of the music again, testing the rhythmic possibilities of "In Time," or dipping back into his Ray Charles roots for his reading of "Que Sera Será," a haunting, eerie, even scary performance of the old Doris Day hit. *Small Talk* (1974), the final album by anything resembling the original group, documents little more than the dissipation of this brilliant career.

By the time the band washed up on the rocks of Radio City Music Hall in January 1975, little was left. Sly's own Dostoevskian descent continued, producing a string of news clippings attesting to minor brushes with the law, mixed with occasional, meager comeback efforts, culminating with his disappearance as a fugitive from justice. Outside of a wobbly, inarticulate appearance accepting the group's induction in the Rock & Roll Hall of Fame at New York's Waldorf Astoria in 1993, he has not been seen in public since.

But long before that, Sly gave up explaining himself. His final interviews were little more than monosyllabic denials of culpability. He eventually just stopped talking. Who can blame him? It has been a long, sorry crawl through unattractive territory for many years for Sly. Dignifying it with discussion hardly seems necessary.

Other people can probably even tell his story better. They say what they saw. They tell what they felt. They knew the heat of the fire and many still bear the scorch marks. To a one, they speak with pride and amazement recollecting their time with Sly, even if they all are far removed from where they were when they first left.

David Kapralik lives in the serene beauty of up-country Maui, where he oversees a flower and onion farm on the slopes of the mystical volcano Haleakala. James Vernon Brown is the host of a public affairs television program and the driving force behind a nonprofit group raising funds to help youth at risk in Salt Lake City, Utah. Stephani Owens is an executive at a civil engineering firm, where they know little of her show business past. Hamp Banks busies himself with a number of enterprises, including his own record label; he ran for mayor of San Francisco and remains a community activist in the Hunters Point neighborhood.

Of the musicians, only Larry Graham vaulted out of the group to any measurable success. His Graham Central Station parlayed the basic Sly and the Family Stone formulas to achieve some modest hits. In the wake of recent funk revivals, Graham, who lives with his wife and family in a Jehovah's Witnesses compound in Jamaica, has re-formed his '70s group and regularly tours European music festivals. He recently added Rose Stone on vocals, and about half of his show is Sly's material. In fact, in 1997, he took Cynthia Robinson and Jerry Martini with the band and appeared on a cable concert telecast hosted by the comedian Sinbad.

Graham seems to have appropriated the legacy.

Martini lives on Waikiki Beach in Honolulu, married to his fifth wife, and recently quit his six-night-a-week job playing sax in the house band at the skyscraper bar overlooking the harbor where he'd worked the previous eight years. Robinson, who admitted she was scuffling, lives with her two grown daughters and her six grandchildren in Sacramento and plays a little in a casual band. Gregg Errico works with a variety of blues and rock bands around the Bay Area.

Freddie Stewart may be the most remote of all. He moved back to Vallejo, where he is the pastor of a church. His father and mother attend the weekly services—they sold the house in San Francisco which their eldest son helped them to buy and returned to Vallejo—along with his sister Vet, who has also moved back to town. By day, he drives a bus for disabled school children in San Francisco.

And Sly? You hear many different stories. Some may even be true. But if you seek to discover what happened, heed his own words: Listen to the voices!

—Joel Selvin, July 1997

THE VOICES
[In Order of Appearance]

ALPHA STEWART: The Queen Mother of the Stewart family, the indefatigable Alpha (yes, she has a sister named Omega) has been married to KC Stewart since she was a teenager in Texas. They met at a church function. She is known among members of the group as "Big Mama."

KC STEWART: The patriarch of the Stewarts cleaned office buildings in downtown Vallejo until his oldest son wrote and produced "C'mon and Swim" for Bobby Freeman. He traveled extensively with Sly and the Family Stone, where his title was "Big Daddy." He says he has never smoked, drunk, or said a cuss word in his life. Nobody doubts that.

VAETTA STEWART: "Little Sister" had the distinction of having a vocal group produced by Sly for his Stone Flower label named after her. Vet, as she is universally known, joined a Berkeley-based gospel group, the Heavenly Tones, as a teenager after recovering from brain surgery. The group came under the wing of Reverend James Cleveland and recorded for Savoy Records. But from the very start of Sly and the Family Stone recording sessions, background vocals were inevitably sung by Little Sister—Vet and her two gospel associates, Elva 'Tiny" Mouton and Mary McCreary, who left the group to marry rock star Leon Russell.

FREDDIE STEWART: KC and Alpha's other son, four years younger than Sylvester, sang and played music with his brother since they were both children. He assumed his brother's stage name and became Freddie Stone when Sly broadcast an invitation to audition for his brother's band over the air on KSOL. Freddie and the Stone Souls contributed both guitarist Freddie and drummer Gregg Errico to the original lineup of Sly and the Family Stone.

SHELBY GIVENS: Married to the late Oakland-based soul singer Odia Coates (best known for her Paul Anka duet, "(You're) Having My Baby"), who also made some Bay Area club appearances backed by a nascent Sly and the Family Stone. Shelby remembers catching the Stewart family gospel group at local churches.

JOHN TURK: He first met Sylvester when the two were children on a Vallejo playground, and they started playing music together as teenagers. Turk served as an older, more experienced role model to teenage Sylvester. Sly left him holding down the stage at the Mission District niterie Little Bo Peep's, where Turk and Sly played together as Sly and the Stoners before Sly took that band's trumpet player, Cynthia Robinson, and departed to form Sly and the Family Stone. He later tapped Turk to be bandleader in the combo that toured behind Little Sister.

HAMP "BUBBA" BANKS: When Sly first met his next role model, Banks was an ex-Marine running a hairstyling salon in the heart of the Fillmore District and pimping as a sideline. He forged a deep bond with the young disc jockey—and took up with his sister, Rose—before briefly disappearing. When he returned, his old friend was living a rock star's life in a Hollywood Hills mansion and Bubba was instantly installed as his ubiquitous, autocratic factotum. He finally married Rose, although they subsequently divorced.

CYNTHIA ROBINSON: Her lifelong devotion to Syl, as she invariably refers to him, began from a distance when Sly spent his senior year of high school with his sister Loretta in Sacramento. She is his most loyal lieutenant. He is the father of one of her two children.

DAVID FROELICH: Sly's junior college music theory instructor left enough of an impression that Sly invariably singled him out for thanks on the backs of album covers throughout his career.

JERRY MARTINI: The self-described band clown first met Sly during his Vallejo doo-wop stage with The Viscaynes. He played in the band on "C'mon and Swim" and repeatedly urged his disc jockey friend to put together a group. He eventually did.

MIKE STEVENS: He barely remembers the details of his brief association with the budding genius, when he and Sly belonged to The Viscaynes together.

BOBBY FREEMAN: San Francisco's first rock and roll star blasted out of Mission High with "Do You Wanna Dance" in

1958, but his star had diminished by the time nineteen-year-old Sly made "C'mon and Swim," the 1964 Top Ten rocker that was Sly's first real hit record.

CARL SCOTT: The young protégé of the extraordinary Tom Donahue learned his craft well at Autumn Records. After he ran off to Los Angeles with Donahue and Mitchell's management clients, he wound up as a well-liked, long-term executive at Warner Brothers Records.

SAL VALENTINO: The Beau Brummels' lead vocalist grew up on the streets of North Beach, where his father used to play stickball with the DiMaggio brothers.

RON ELLIOTT: He was Lennon to Valentino's McCartney in the Brummels—alternately witty and sullen, whimsical and acerbic—and it showed in his songcraft.

DARBY SLICK: The lead guitarist in the Great Society is best known for having written a song that his then sister-in-law took with her when she joined Jefferson Airplane, "Somebody to Love."

GRACE SLICK: When she left the Great Society to join the already-established Jefferson Airplane, the band she had formed with her husband and brother-in-law fell apart. Their excruciating experience in the studio with Sly didn't help.

ALAN SCHULTZ: With his partner Les Molloy, he hired a young, inexperienced Sly—fresh out of a commercial radio school—as a prime-time deejay on their upstart radio station, KSOL. Within a year, Sly had practically single-handedly dislodged the monolithic Black radio station KDIA from soul supremacy in Oakland and the rest of the Bay Area.

JOHNNY MORRIS: The veteran soul radio man started his career in the shadow of Sly on KSOL and followed him to KDIA, where Morris established himself as one of the leading broadcasters in Black radio.

LARRY GRAHAM: Originally a guitar player who worked with a variety of rhythm and blues bands on the thriving Oakland scene of the mid-sixties, Graham was playing bass in a popular nightclub duo with his mother, Dell Graham, when Sly heard him play. With Sly and the Family Stone, Graham rewrote the language of his instrument.

JAMES VERNON "J.B." BROWN: A graduate of the University of California, J.B. was working for Chevron Oil when he first met Sly. He and Hamp Banks moved together to Los Angeles to form a kind of personal staff for Sly, although J.B. ended up cutting a solo album and launching an abortive attempt to crash the charts on his own.

GREGG ERRICO: A chance meeting with Freddie Stone flaunting his notoriety as brother of the disc jockey led to Errico joining the ghetto R&B outfit Freddie and the Stone Souls when he was just a knobby-kneed White teenager fresh out of high school. He became the first original member of Sly and the Family Stone to leave the band.

MICKEY HART: The Grateful Dead drummer was running a drum store with his father in nearby San Carlos when he caught Sly and the Family Stone at Winchester Cathedral.

DAVID KAPRALIK: A Columbia Records executive with a distinguished career (he signed Barbra Streisand, Andy Williams, Cassius Clay), the elfin fanatic led Sly and the Family Stone from the after-hours scene in Redwood City to the peak of the music business.

CLIVE DAVIS: The lion of the record industry was starting his career as president of Epic Records when Sly and the Family Stone were signed. By the time Sly was one of the company's biggest-selling acts, Davis had ascended to the top post at the parent company, CBS Records.

AL DEMARINO: The agent signed Sly and the Family Stone to the prestigious William Morris Agency and stood stalwart sentry duty through thick and thin. He dabbled in the backstage intrigue that led to the departure of manager Kapralik.

STEPHANI OWENS: She was Stephani Swanigan when she served as Sly's first personal assistant, a relationship that blurred the boundaries of personal and professional. Her efficiency and intelligence were often the lone outposts of sanity in the midst of a world gone mad.

STEPHEN PALEY: The distant relative of the CBS founder first met Sly as a photographer but later was assigned to work with Sly and the Family Stone when he came aboard the artist and repertoire department of Epic Records. He was the best man at Sly's Madison Square Garden wedding.

STEVE TOPLEY: The first record this veteran promotion man worked was "Splish Splash," by Bobby Darin. The former Navy frogman promoted all of Sly's records to radio, first as a promotion man for Epic Records and later directly in the employ of Sly's Stone Flower Productions.

KITSAUN KING: The daughter of blues singer Saunders King moved to Los Angeles after her sister, Debbie, became romantically involved with Sly. She lived, on and off, at his Hollywood homes and worked at the Stone Flower offices.

VERNON "MOOSE" CONSTAN: A high school friend of the Errico brothers, Constan was an electronics whiz who hot-rodded all Sly's early equipment and trooped the gear from gig to gig.

ELVA "TINY" MOUTON: One of the Heavenly Tones, Tiny Mouton, Vaetta ("Little Sister") Stewart, and Mary McCreary sang on Sly and the Family Stone records from the very beginning, long before Sly began producing the girls under the group name Little Sister.

BOBBY WOMACK: The veteran rhythm and blues heavyweight fell into the Sly Stone scene when they were both at the top of their games, often collaborating on each other's recording projects.

EDWARD ("EDDIE CHIN") ELLIOTT: A longtime friend of Hamp Banks, Eddie Chin was a successful career criminal who spent time hanging around the Sly camp with Bubba, eventually marrying Sly's sister Vet.

KEN ROBERTS: Manager of Frankie Valli and the Four Seasons, the show business entrepreneur started out producing Sly and the Family Stone concerts when nobody else would, but soon supplanted Kapralik as manager of all the group's affairs.

ROBERT JOYCE: The sound technician was a nineteen-year-old from Buffalo, New York, when he signed on as Sly's production manager at the height of the juggernaut. He left Sly to work for many years with David Bowie.

PAT RIZZO: Jazz saxist and relative to Sinatra crony Jilly Rizzo, "The Rizz" was hired to intimidate Jerry Martini, who was asking embarrassing questions about money he was owed, and stayed around to become close friends with Martini anyway.

KATHLEEN SILVA: She met Sly when she was a teenager. They had a child, Sylvester Bubb Ali Stewart Jr. Nine months later, they were married before a capacity crowd at Madison Square Garden. Five months after that, they were in divorce court.

RUSTY ALLEN: The nineteen-year-old bass player who used to watch Sly wipe mucus off his lip during television performances stepped straight from the Oakland nightclub scene into Larry Graham's shoes in Sly and the Family Stone as the whole trip was peaking.

TOM FLYE: The engineer who happened to remix Sly's live tracks for the crucial Woodstock album was working at the Record Plant in Sausalito when Sly checked in to finish *Fresh*. Flye remained with Sly for several years.

ONE

A LITTLE PRINCE

KC and Alpha Stewart at Sly's wedding.

ALPHA STEWART: I think Syl was born with a big voice. When he was about five, we went to San Francisco and the bishop put him up on the table, so people could see him. He had such a big voice. And that was more than once. Oh, yes. There was this time in Berkeley one Sunday afternoon, when Syl was singing. They had this balcony, and this lady started shouting. They had to get her down from there so she wouldn't fall, and they had to hold Syl and tell him to shut up and stop singing.

My kids could always sing. Loretta could always play music. She started taking music from a lady, but after a while, Loretta ended up teaching her. She was probably about thirteen or fourteen years old. It was a built-in thing. The kids were always singing. They had a group called the Stewart Four—Loretta, Syl, Freddie, and Rose. Vet wasn't born yet.

This one day we went down to Stockton to sing in a church. They took up a collection for the kids. That day in Stockton, Syl saw a man playing guitar. We received eighteen dollars, and Syl said, "Mama, if you take my share of the money and buy a guitar, I'll play just like that man." The next day, his daddy went down to the secondhand store and bought an old guitar. When he came home from school that evening, he just fell out, had a fit. I took that guitar and tuned it. And Syl made fun of my tuning. So his daddy went down to the music shop on Tennessee Street in Vallejo, to see how they tuned guitars. And I had it tuned exactly right. But Syl thought I was nuts. Ever since then Sylvester been playing the guitar. He must have been about nine. He was just a kid. He wasn't big enough to carry his own instrument.

KC STEWART: My daddy was a musician. He used to play like Roy Clark, Grand Ole Opry kind of stuff.

ALPHA STEWART: His daddy used to play the violin for dances and stuff like that. Somehow that old violin ended up here in Vallejo. But it's just a music thing. All the kids could play. Rose never had a lesson. And Vet, she plays organ now for the church, and she never had a lesson in her life.

VAETTA STEWART: Mama taught Sly how to tune the guitar. Daddy made a drum with a washboard, and we just went from there. I came along last, so a lot of that happened before I got here. I just remember Loretta playing and singing, that's as far back as I can go. All of us. After dinner, before dinner, during dinner, in the car, on the way to church, after church.

ALPHA STEWART: We went down to Bakersfield, and a preacher wanted to record them. Syl must have been about eleven years old. Loretta wasn't there, but my niece—they were about the same age—said she would play. They had about three or four songs they made. At that time it was 78s. That was the Stewart Four.

FREDDIE STEWART: We made a record, had a red label, and there was one song that Sly sang lead called "On the Battlefield." I remember driving to Texas, must have been 1958, taking our records down there to sell them. Each one had to be individually wrapped. We went to churches and sang down there. We had relatives. Most of our people are in Texas. We'd go down there and stay and maybe with some kinfolk in Bakersfield on the way back. Selling records, that type of thing. We were always in church. If it wasn't with the family, I was singing in the choir. The pastor in Vallejo was my uncle, married to my mother's sister.

SHELBY GIVENS: I would see the Stewarts perform on occasion, sometimes on Sunday afternoons when churches would get together, or sometimes late at night when certain churches would have late services. It was a family of kids with a lot of musical talent in the family. Sly's guitar and keyboard talent were probably the things I observed first before I heard him sing. I remember his playing was very outstanding. That's how a family made their mark on the gospel scene.

The most central thing to the whole religious practices of the Church of God in Christ was the emphasis on the transformation experience that they refer to as the holy ghost. It was that transforming experience that really made you a full bona fide member. And they usually regarded the evidence of that experience by speaking in tongues. You could not succeed in the world, because worldliness was seen as something that was a form of departure from God, from righteousness, and, by definition, that meant that you in a sense were kind of doomed. So when people backslid, there was almost a compulsion to take on attributes of worldliness—alcohol, tobacco, nightclubbing, dancing, adultery—a whole range of things associated with the unrighteous. You could not have any respectability anywhere in the middle. If you sin, you're going to hell anyway, so you might as well taste it all.

JOHN TURK: I used to go see him at the Church of God in Christ. I used to go to the church and listen to the band. All I remember is Sly and the piano player. I would sit outside and listen. It was just Black gospel music and he would be like playing the blues over that. In Vallejo, he was the only guy playing the guitar in the churches that I knew of. His whole thing came from the gospel church, his outlook toward music, because when I started playing with him, he didn't know no jazz tunes. He was just real talented.

FREDDIE STEWART: There was the Cherrybusters. There was the Royal Aces. That was another group. They wore white jackets with a black ace on the sleeve. He didn't do a lot of stuff. He was just cool. He was with some guys that just liked to be cool. He had his first car, an old Buick, light green Dynaflow with the trunk darker green. He named it the Booty Green. It was immaculate.

JOHN TURK: He was one of a group, the Cherrybusters, in high school. They wore orange jackets. It wasn't a gang, just a group of guys, all good-looking. Sly was playing his guitar then, and he had a light green '53 Chevy, except the trunk, which was dark green. He called it Booty Green.

HAMP "BUBBA" BANKS: Being Black, it makes a great story—"I was poverty ridden, we ate out of the garbage can." Then people say, "This poor kid, he made it." Sly was looking for that. But his sister used to tell me he was in this club called the Cherrybusters—bad guys, he was in it. You know why he was in it? He had a car. Nobody else had a car.

FREDDIE STEWART: We didn't ever lack anything. A lot of things I would get handed down because Sly is four years older. There was a time that I wanted a certain type of shirt, a Pendleton shirt. My mother said that she would go to a store or thrift shop and get a Pendleton shirt. What she would actually do is she would get me wool shirts and put Pendleton labels in the shirt. The girls needed something, they got it. When Sly was old enough to get a car, he got a car.

JOHN TURK: I was in a group called the Royal Aces whose lead singer was Jesse James. There was a group called the Webs and there was another group Sly played with whose lead singer was Jimmy Terrell. When we did the talent shows the first time, we kicked everybody's behind because we had a band and they didn't. The other group that was really good was the Webs. They were good, but they didn't have a band. Then Jimmy Terrell came along and he had Sly. We didn't have a guitar, and at that time, '58 or '59, Jimmy McCracklin's song "The Walk" was happening. They got out there and did that song and kicked our behinds. So what we did is we got Sly. That is how I started associating with him, musically. Then Sly hurt his leg and he couldn't play with us for a while and the next thing I knew, he was with The Viscaynes—Charlene Imhoff, Mike Stevens. We all went to the same junior high school. It was more of a vocal group than anything else, and Sly added that flavor to it. They were a good group. Somebody wanted to cut a record of them. Then he went to school in Sacramento for a while.

CYNTHIA ROBINSON: He got kicked out of all the schools in Vallejo for whatever reason, so he came to Sacramento to finish his senior year and stay with his sister Loretta. Before that, I remember when he used to come up and visit. He would be in the choir—his mom and dad would bring him down. The leaders started a car club for all the young men who had cars, so that they had something to do, 'cause they were peeling out in the street at all hours of the night. He was a member of the car club and the choir. He was observant, very quiet, mannerful, and respectful. He never said a lot of useless things. He seemed to be very intelligent, and I never saw him act like a crazy teenager.

DAVID FROELICH: Eventually, we got our own campus up-county where it is now about 1961. It became Solano Community College. We had a choir, a band, the whole bit. My main interest was music theory. What Sly was interested in. His name was Sylvester Stewart; there wasn't any Sly at that point. He was a standout because of his extreme interest in the subject. He was real gone on learning music. He wasn't in any way taken up with professionalism yet. He had a group and he played around locally. I found out he had this voice, so I said, "Hey, you want to sing in the choir?" He signed up for choir. But his main thrust was to take this music theory. He worked real hard and would stay after class. We got to know each other. There was considerable work to be done at home, writing of music and so forth. His work was always excellent. An A student. He would always be in school.

JERRY MARTINI: I met Sly back in '59 or '60. Joe Piazza brought him over for a rehearsal. This was back in the day when Dick Clark was very popular and San Francisco had its own Dick Clark named Dick Stewart and his show "The KPIX Dance Party." Joe Piazza was a regular on the show and so was Sly. He was very collegiate looking, he had his hair parted on the side. He had a singing group called The Viscaynes. We met each other and immediately hit it off. We had this eye contact thing. Sly had this energy happening. We hit it off as friends immediately. The Viscaynes were a Vallejo singing group that was very hip and very unique because it was an integrated band. They had a Filipino. Sly was the Afro. There were girls and boys and different colors.

ALPHA STEWART: They were an all-White group. Syl was the only fly in that buttermilk.

MIKE STEVENS: We sang slow rock and roll songs. There were two girls, Charlene Imhoff and Maria Boldway. And there was Frank Arellano and Charles Gebhart. Sly was a Black guy among middle-class White kids. In some ways, Sly may have felt a little more connected to Frank, who was Filipino, because they were not White. But there was no tension between Sly and the White members. In Vallejo at that time, there was just one high school, and everybody went to high school together, the Blacks, and Whites, and whoever else was around.

JERRY MARTINI: He had a hell of a time back then because when he was in The Viscaynes, he was hammering one of the girls in the band, the most beautiful girl, and they had to keep it secret. He had all this talent and was so far beyond this racial bullshit that was going on back then that it had to affect his psyche a little bit. It was just bullshit. He was a good-looking, talented young man and the girls in the band fell for him. They had to sneak around. When I met him, he was hanging with Joe Piazza. I played with Joe Piazza and the Continentals. We started doing side gigs together. It was a real Top 40 band. Sly played bass and sang; he hadn't started playing keyboards yet. We did a few gigs down on Broadway.

BOBBY FREEMAN: I met Sly in 1962. I was doing a show in Vallejo and he had a band. I don't recall the name of the band, but it was his band. At the time, Sly had a record out I don't think anybody is familiar with called "Yellow Moon." I was impressed with him and he had this horn player, one of the first ever I saw that played trumpet and organ. His name is John Turk, a phenomenal musician who never really got the breaks. How Sly and Bob Mitchell and Tom Donahue hooked up, I don't know, but that's what started the ball rolling.

JERRY MARTINI: We were the backup band and we also did Sly's first record, "Yellow Moon" [backed with] "Uncle Sam Needs You Boy." It didn't get off the ground. Sly sang lead on both sides. He sang high on one side and low on the other side. He had incredible range. It was just a single, but it got him the attention of Bob Mitchell and Tom Donahue, who hired him to work at Autumn Records. When Sly was nineteen in 1963, he wrote "C'mon and Swim" for Bobby Freeman and had his first gold record.

Sly and Donahue.

CARL SCOTT: Donahue was bigger than life. He was a huge, huge, huge figure—both as a man and a mind. He had a presence that demanded you pay attention to what he had to say. I always thought of a young Orson Welles. He was very big, very impressive, very smart. I loved listening to him. He always had wonderful opinions. I always thought he was fair and a sweet person. Great guy. And what a voice. You shut up and you listened. Whatever the topic, he knew everything about it—politics, music, movies, plays. Mitchell was wiry and somewhat snotty. Where Donahue was suave and debonair, Mitchell was a street guy. Somewhere in the back of Mitchell's mind I think he thought of himself as a gangster. Black leather jacket, black jeans. Very caustic. He was a sharp radio disc jockey. What one didn't know, the other did. Mitchell was a gambler and Donahue was a thinker. Mitchell was more of the moment and Donahue saw the big picture. Mitchell knew rock and roll—he knew what was hip, what was cool, happening—and Mitchell could pick a hit.

They were at KYA. Mitchell went to work at KYA in the afternoon and Donahue did six to nine. They had a time slot that was pretty important in Top 40 radio, a six-hour shift, one right into the other. They decided that as long as they had that shift and had that influence on records, they'd do some promotion, record hops and things like that. They wanted to make some money, so they started setting up record hops, started hitting on all the various record companies to send acts up to San Francisco to play their record hops. That started to work for them. They started to do some promotion around the Bay Area, some very small record hops at Redwood City, up at Rio Nido, during the summer. They were ninety-nine-cent things. I would pick the acts up and cart them around. They'd get three, four, five hundred people at Redwood City and make a few bucks. That dovetailed into a few other promotions, Peter, Paul and Mary at the Masonic Auditorium. It got a tiny bit bigger and they started to make a little bit more money. They decided to put together a record company and they formed Autumn Records.

BOBBY FREEMAN: I knew Bob and Tom from Philadelphia, where they'd have these record hops. Whenever you had a new record out, to get exposure and airplay, you would go to these record hops on Friday and Saturday nights and lip-synch your records. That would initially assure you some play. So I knew them before they came to the Bay Area. In San Francisco, they were number one on KYA. They did well. They brought shows to the Cow Palace. They did very well as far as the record business. I think Tom eventually bought a ranch with some horses and Bob used to like to go to the racetrack and bet on the horses. But I'd be the first to say, they looked out for me.

We used to do these shows at the Cow Palace. One was called the Twist show, one was the Limbo show. I think Bob and Tom did about three shows at the Cow Palace. There were no big rock and roll shows there at the time; we established a record as far as attendance. I think all three of the shows drew something like 17,600 people, if I remember correctly. Any act that was any act made their way to the Cow Palace for Bob Mitchell and Tom Donahue. And Sly was their bandleader. They put together a record company called Autumn Records and Sly was the producer of most of the stuff that got put together on that label, including my stuff.

CARL SCOTT: The Cow Palace was a real fluke. It had never been their intention to go into the Cow Palace. It was just a stroke of luck that happened. Tom was talking to the fellow who ran Cameo-Parkway. They gave him Chubby Checker for a weekend—our little gift to you—and Donahue went out looking for venues. He wanted to find a place to present Chubby Checker. He came back to the office and said, "I just booked the Cow Palace" and Mitchell said "What? Are you crazy?" So they put on the first Cow Palace show and Chubby Checker was the headliner. They decided to hit on all the record companies and get acts to appear on that concert. The first Cow Palace show, Phil Spector conducted the band and Sly put together the sidemen.

BOBBY FREEMAN: There's always been a little rival thing between myself and Chubby Checker. He was headlining the show at the Cow Palace. The place was jam-packed. "C'mon and Swim" hadn't been recorded yet. I was determined to blow the top off this place. They called me back for an encore. I didn't have anything prepared. I started out by saying, "I'm going to show you some new dances." I started creating these things called the Basketball Twist, the Tennis Twist and all of a sudden, my arms started moving and my bottom part started shaking and I said, "And this is called The Swim." All I wanted was to make Chubby come out and work harder. Sly said, "Hey, man, what was that dance you were doin'? You got a new dance."

"C'mon and Swim" was the first thing we did. I created the dance in 1961 and I went to Hawaii to do some shows. When I got back things had changed. This young lady named Judy Mac who worked at the Galaxie basically was getting credit for doing my dance that I started doing in my act when I was working North Beach in 1962. Tom Donahue said the best way to solve that problem is to do a record. So we brought it to Sly. Sly wrote the song.

Bobby Freeman, Cow Palace, 1962.

CARL SCOTT: I know that Donahue had something to do with the writing of "C'mon and Swim." Sly and Donahue are credited as writers. Donahue actually contributed lyrically and Sly musically. I don't think anybody expected it to be a big success. But "C'mon and Swim" came out and, in short order, it seemed to just become a big summer record.

JERRY MARTINI: On the record, Sly is playing organ, guitar, and bass. "The Swim" was a million-seller and the album was very big also. I was just in the band, I wasn't special. He had about a fifteen-piece band. Big band, a big fat horn section. Sly is playing all these instruments and he did great.

BOBBY FREEMAN: Sly is playing organ, guitar, and I think his brother Freddie was playing bass. He produced it himself. He was very bright, music savvy, educated—he had everything all in one hat. Outgoing. There was no heavy partying, just normal. But we enjoyed what we were doing. We were friends before we even went in to do "The Swim." We lived not that far away from each other. When he moved to San Francisco and got his first apartment, it was maybe twenty-five minutes away from where I was living. On Haight, nice place, between Gough and Laguna.

JERRY MARTINI: Sly was probably the most brilliant musician around. All we did was smoke pot and drink wine, but he was really an intense person. With the money that he got from "C'mon and Swim," he put a down payment on the house at 700 Urbano. He didn't pay for that house—Daddy did—but he put down the down payment. He went from Vallejo to this beautiful home on Urbano Street.

KC STEWART: I worked for a while, commuting back and forth. Sometimes, weekends, Sly would come to work with me. Freddie, too. They were really good when I got a call.

ALPHA STEWART: They all learned how to work. They knew what it is to clean the toilet, wash walls. They could all cook a little bit. They had to learn.

CARL SCOTT: [Sly] was a baby then. He was just a young man, a kid. Mitchell felt that Sly was almost like a little prince. He was very musical all the time. He was always singing, always humming, messing around with drumsticks. There was always a certain kind of young hipness to him. He was constantly the musician. He was a rock and roll guy. He was certainly not what we consider to be R&B. He had a pop sensibility to him and that was always obvious. He was so young and so cool and so nice. He had a Beatle haircut and it was either brown or red or somewhere in between. Tight black pants, Beatle boots, short hair. Wore glasses. I remember when they bought him his first car, a green Jaguar XKE. I used to write his paychecks—he didn't earn a lot. But they took care of Sly. They knew that Sly was a genius or could be. They did not take advantage of Sly in any way. They knew that Sly could do wonderful things.

FREDDIE STEWART: I did a lot of sessions. I didn't do hardly any playing. I did a lot of singing. A lot of times it was jingles for jeans. I did some playing for the Beau Brummels.

SAL VALENTINO: We [Beau Brummels] were down playing the Morocco Room in the summer of 1964. He came with Tom, Bob, and Carl Scott. That's when we first met Sly. We knew a little bit about the records he done with Bobby. Tom commenced to pursue us to getting signed and told us Sly was going to be our producer. We were all thrilled to be making records. We went in the studio with Sly and we made "Laugh Laugh," "Just a Little," "Still In Love With You Baby," all the first album.

RON ELLIOTT: He was fun to work with. He would be dancing around. He brought the band up a notch. In those days, he was clear-minded. He was involved body and soul. I can still see him dancing behind the control booth window, laughing. He had me do a lot of over-dubs, playing different parts, acoustic parts, electric parts.

SAL VALENTINO: The only experience we had in recording was going down to Gold Star and doing this demo that turned on Tom and got them to come down and see us. So being in the studio, we were kinda in awe of it all and we were mild-mannered, nice neighborhood guys. But Sly had this real enthusiasm, this energy that helped us a lot. We were probably a little apprehensive, a little scared, and Sly broke that down. He was always joking, always real enthusiastic. He wanted to play more than he actually got to play. That just didn't work out. I think the end of "Just a Little" is the only thing he ever did that you can hear, that little timbales thing. He'd show us things. Ron was a little apprehensive about having him play. Ron was into having us do it all. He may have helped with parts from time to time. He didn't do anything on the record. But he pretty much got the most out of us. He did those first records.

DARBY SLICK: Tom Donahue had an open audition, sort of a cattle call, at the nightclub he owned with Bobby Mitchell, Mother's. Sly was already working for Donahue, producing. The Great Society went down to this open audition and played with a bunch of bands, one after another. Afterwards Sly and Donahue came over and said they were real interested in the band. In fact, they were just immediately talking about signing us. They wanted us to come in the studio and record all the songs we played so they could get an overview of the thing. He started coming over to some rehearsals and started having ideas how we should change this and that. We flatly refused to do anything he suggested because we knew where it was at. We didn't want to take any correction from anybody. Getting in the studio was a real nightmare for him and not that much fun for us, because we wouldn't accept any of his ideas there, either. He brought Billy Preston in—he'd been playing with Ray Charles, so we were really impressed with him. I started to go to some sessions that he was producing with the Beau Brummels and some of those other guys, so I started to see more of his musicianship. The more I saw of that side of him, the more I started to take his ideas seriously. He'd sit down at the drums and play, and he was a really good drummer. Or the bass. Or anything you wanted to play, he seemed to be able to play.

The first thing we did, we went into the studio and played everything we knew. Then we went to work on a couple of songs in more detail. "Somebody to Love" took something like fifty takes. It just went on and on and Sly left. We went into the studio and tested everything. We played the song and we thought we killed it. We put everything we had into it. The guy said, "Okay, now I've got the dials right—do another take." We said, "What do you mean? That was the take." He said, "No, I didn't record it." That's what set off that whole chain. We were young and inexperienced and we had sort of blown our wad. We kept doing it and doing it until we got something. I'm sure he thought of us as very unprofessional, unpolished, maybe even not real musicians. And we thought of him as this controlling guy who wanted to make everything be a certain way.

GRACE SLICK: He walked around and played all the instruments. He was amazing. David Miner decided he could sing more easily lying down. He sang some takes lying down on a couch with the microphone bent down.

CARL SCOTT: [Donahue and Mitchell] were having success. They wanted to cash in on their success. They had the Bobby Freeman success. They had the Beau Brummels. They sold to Warner Brothers. They wanted the money. Of course, by that time, they were over the top. They were in debt. They had a racing stable. They were living good. That other electricity took over. They were really grooving. Both of them were spending lots of money.

ALAN SCHULTZ: Les Molloy, my partner at KSOL, and I hired Sly. He was just being converted from Sylvester to Sly. He was referred by somebody on the staff. He was really a bright guy, very animated, very adaptable. During conversation, rather than come on like someone from the ghetto, he really came on as very sophisticated. He could sit and converse with you, on whatever terms you wanted to talk with him on. He was a good-looking guy. He had a good appearance, very sharp dresser. Stations in those days like KSOL were really race stations. The music that we played was Black music. The top stations in the market like KFRC didn't play our music and we didn't play theirs. KDIA was more of the older Black establishment sound. At KSOL, Sly was the one, in many ways, that we counted on to be the vanguard of music.

JOHNNY MORRIS: When I met him the first time, he was working full time at KSOL and I was working part time. The first time I was on the air, April 1964, he had been there for about five or six months. He just graduated from some popular radio school, the Chris Borden School. Before I had a chance to work there at the station, I'd listened to him. He was working seven to midnight. My first impression when I heard him on the air before meeting him, he sounded like a young Tom Donahue. When I had a chance to meet him, he was a lot younger than he sounded on the air. Initially, those first few months, he was sort of doing his regular air stuff, not anything out of the ordinary, stuff you would expect just out of radio school. He was overly aware of his enunciation of words and like that. He didn't really go too far out doing front and back announcing of the songs, as compared to what he branched into later in his deejay style.

As it went on, there was more personality. He would say more things about the records. They started adding more features on his show, like dedications. The dedications, I think, were really unique. No one I had ever heard handled the dedications the way he would. He just had a way of being able to talk with people. He was a fun guy to talk with. He'd start his thing—"Sly with the soul line." He would always come up with unique liners and different things that he created. He told me one time, Tom Johnson, who was the operations manager there at the time, wanted to use the name Sly Sloan, something like that. But it was really Sly who wanted to use the name Sly Stone.

HAMP "BUBBA" BANKS: I was a hairstylist at Huff's Fashionette on Fillmore and Geary. He came in, and at the time, he was a deejay, and that is all he was to me—a little deejay. The shop that I worked in catered to pimps and whores, guys that got their hair dipped—that was the in thing at the time. I never noticed him, really. I just knew he was a little square that was on the radio. He came in one day and got into an argument. Somebody said something smart to him and he reacted in a way that made me think that this cat has got some heart. I thought this cat can run with me if he can handle himself like that. We hooked up. He was working nights and I was working days. I did hair every day. His show was off at midnight. I would go to the radio station. I would do his spots because he always wanted to relate to pimping and the streets. I had ladies of the evening, whatever. I was in the streets. I would do things when the break came on; "This is Hamp da Bubba da Banks saying don't touch that dial until you get hip to the soul style" or "Sly, you come on and rap, I gotta go check my trap." Just all the street slang, I put all that part to his radio show.

JOHNNY MORRIS: Station manager Tom Johnson was a genius at creating certain things that had not been done in radio, such as the KSOL Soul Brothers, the call letters KSOL. They had the Red, Hot and Blue Soul Forty-Five Survey. They had jingles. They did unique things, like the traveling soul show where you write-in your favorite jock and he would come to your house and do a show. With Sly on at night, for that first year, they just swamped KDIA, even though KDIA had more power at five thousand watts, versus KSOL, which had two hundred and fifty watts at night. Sly pulled something like 40 percent of the target audience. Whatever he would do, even though it was not within the boundaries of what he was supposed to do, they would just say, "Well, that is Sly."

His show opened with Lord Buckley going, "Hey all you cats and kitties." Then a girl's voice says, "I'm talking about Sly Stone." He had little voices he would do—"cook, Sly, cook, smoke." His favorite artist at that time was Ray Charles, which if you really listen to Sly in his early stuff you can hear. Billy Preston used to come up to the station a lot because Sly collaborated with Billy on one of his albums called *Wildest Organ in Town!*

Sly did a jingle package that they used on the station, and those were some of Billy's rhythm tracks. A lot of the stuff that he did in the studio with Billy Preston he used for his own jingles: "I'm the one that they call the Rolling Stone." Billy would come around the time that Sly would get off, around eleven o'clock. I was working the midnight shift then, so I would see him when they both left. I think at that time, too, Sly was also playing out in North Beach.

HAMP "BUBBA" BANKS: When we got off the show at twelve o'clock, we'd go to North Beach. We would put on our suits. Every night, we were the two players of North Beach. He was known to the people that were the night life, the North Beach people. But I was the guy after two o'clock in the morning, the streets. Up until two o'clock in the morning was the entertainment and the glamour. He had that covered and I had the other part covered, so we could go anywhere. Once we left the clubs at two o'clock and went to Pam-Pam's or Original Joe's, it was me and him. We might bring a party, but we were the center of attraction. My life is what he was fascinated with—he wanted to be that tough guy and I was that tough guy. Not that I did anything tough, I just knew the game.

Sly knew who I was, but his set didn't because it was all fun and games with them. [Sly bandmate] Don Wehr either said something or did something. He just was running off at the mouth.

I told Sly, "I'm going to punch him in his mouth." I drove over to Sly's and parked my car and walked in. As much as his people couldn't stand me, they all had to accept me. That was the beauty of it. They had to play like they liked me. I walked in and Sly said that Don Wehr was there. I walked straight in and he looked up at me and I smacked him in the mouth. His involvement was not street. I was street.

TWO

REALLY A RHYTHM AND BLUES CAT

Sly studio portrait, 1968.

LARRY GRAHAM: There were clubs around the Bay Area that were popular during that time, Sportmen's Club, Showcase. They had a club over in Richmond, they had a club in Menlo Park, Black Cat. They had one on Seventh and Wood, Esther's Orbit Room, and there was this other place called the Embassy Club on Wood. During those times there was a lot of outlets you could play. It proved to be a training ground. I played all those clubs. The Whispers were around; they wore matching uniforms and so forth. Remember a group called The Ballads? They were around; they wore uniforms. Of course, probably the Temptations was influencing a lot of people at that time, getting the steps and the routines and all that stuff.

CYNTHIA ROBINSON: I used to play with Jimmy McCracklin and Lowell Fulsom. I used to hear all these guys on 78s at my mother's when I was a teenager. When my friends came in with these 45s, I said I didn't even want to hear about it. Seventy-eights were the thing for me. I used to daydream that I was onstage playing the solos; I'm playing with B. B. King and I'm playing with Lowell Fulsom, with Jimmy McCracklin. And I literally ended up being in a band that backed them up at different clubs. It was like a dream come true, but that was as big as I could dream.

JERRY MARTINI: I had already met The Beatles. I had already been to Europe. I already had an album out, didn't make it, but I had already played [television's] *Shindig*. I had already made a movie with Connie Stevens and Dean Jones by the time the band started. So I had the most experience. I was also in a unique band called George and Teddy and the Condors. We were at the Condor. Before then, I played at Pierre's with Ricky and the Red Tops. George and Teddy would come over and see us. They were doing very well at the Condor. They liked the way I played sax. I used to dance on the bar—I've always been a clown. They hired me and I became a Condor. We went all over.

Our managers sent us to Italy to make it. That was like sending somebody to the Dark Ages.

During that time, we were doing the Mashed Potato and all those hip dances. But when we went to Italy in 1965, they were still doing the Twist—at least five years behind as far as music and their dances. They booked us in this club in Rome and there was this sister club called the Riviera. It was fun, but it was also kind of a nightmare because it was so backwards and the customs were so different. Plus, we were four White guys backing up two Black singers, which was unheard of in Italy. They are not prejudiced, they just don't consider Black people. They used to call the guys in the band *due negro*, which means two Blacks. The Beatles had just come out. I had my picture with The Beatles. We were playing this nightclub that you had to wear a tuxedo to get in and The Beatles came in. John was wearing this captain's hat. Paul was with this beautiful Italian hooker. I never got to meet him.

GREGG ERRICO: Leon Patillo had a group called the V.I.P.s. They were the hot group in town, soul band, and they used to play at the YMCA and all the big dances. When his drummer was sick, he'd call me. One night, there was this guy, Freddie Stewart, who was the brother of Sly Stone, the disc jockey that was on KSOL at the time. We played a couple sets and Freddie introduced himself and we got to talking. That night after the gig, Freddie came up to me and asked if I was interested in doing something with him. About a week or two after that, we got together at Freddie's house, which was also Sly's house out on Urbano Street, where his folks live, and we started rehearsing. We started getting gigs. We were together for maybe a year, a little under a year—Freddie and the Stone Souls.

FREDDIE STEWART: We had one uniform that we wore: vest, pants, a shirt. We entered a contest that they had out at the Cow Palace and won. We started taking the gigs over because we had a lot of fun. Sometimes we'd come out and we'd dress up as old women. In fact, we had to do it a couple of times. We were playing at this club called Little Bo Peep's on Mission. At the time we were playing at this particular club, Cynthia, who my brother knew, was in my brother's group, called Sly and the Stoners. Sly would get off the air and come and play at this very same club that I was playing.

CYNTHIA ROBINSON: Freddie was playing with his group, Freddie and the Stone Souls. They had these wild outfits on with big, wide black-and-white checkers, and pink pants. I was going to ask Freddie for a job. But when he walked up the stairs with his band and looked at me like, "Who the hell is she?" I thought, "Quit being an introvert." They played, and I mean they were cooking. He's the one who whipped them into shape, because some of those musicians really couldn't play. But he knew exactly what to have them play, what order. He knew how to orchestrate the harmony to where it had the biggest, fattest sound. And he had them stepping high to the songs. They were cooking. I watched the show and went, "Woo, I'd like to ask these guys for a gig." But I didn't have the nerve.

So I went back to Richmond, and a couple of days later or a week later, my boyfriend told me Sly was coming to the house. I said, "Why?" And he said Sly wanted to talk to us about something, or me about something. I thought maybe it's about the record. Because I played on the show, I did a few little numbers.

So when he came, we were in the garage, and Syl came through the house. His aura was forceful, but he was so gentle that I knew that this was something different. It was like a change in your life is getting ready to happen, maybe, if you take advantage of it.

This was a group called Sly and the Stoners. And he had these great big Great Danes I was afraid of. I left my daughter on the floor when he brought them to rehearsal. He brought them into the room, I jumped up on the B-3 organ, and I left my little baby on the floor. This was in a club, getting ready to rehearse. As a disc jockey, he had clubs where he booked entertainers. He always had his hand into more than one thing. I don't know how he kept it all together, but it seemed like he was happiest doing that. He always had to have a bunch of things to do and he could handle it well. Could always keep it balanced.

JOHN TURK: I had been playing with Johnny Heartsman. We played in Vegas with LaVern Baker. We went there, once with Johnny Heartsman, and when we got ready to go the second time, John was having some problems. He decided that he didn't want to go and we wanted more money. LaVern started to hire us without John, so when we came back, in order for us to keep working, I bought an organ and I started playing at the Chi-Chi Club in a band called the Young Lions. Sly called and he said, "Remember that band we were talking about getting together—are we going to do it or not?" The first rehearsal, we went to Sly's house and he brought out a bunch of albums and throws them on the floor. He says, "Pick out a character." He had The Beatles, The Turtles, and all that. We were jazz cats, at least we thought we were. What does that have to do with music? He was ahead of his time. He wanted a show, not just a musical band. He wanted us to wear pajamas to the gig. I did buy me some long boots and I did grow a goatee.

We were playing at Little Bo Peep's out in the Mission District. He was still doing the disc jockey thing and he didn't really show up until one o'clock. We weren't doing original tunes—just covers, all R&B. Even though he was in the rock and roll scene, he was really a rhythm and blues cat. I know his riffs were from rhythm and blues. He'd come in and see Johnny Talbot—at that time, he was the funkiest band in the Bay Area, period. His following was more from him being on the radio. He was quite a figure in the Bay then. He had a lot of pretty ladies. He had the XKE.

FREDDIE STEWART: He painted the car disc jockey purple. Beautiful.

JAMES VERNON "J.B." BROWN: Little Bo Peep's I would say was the emergence of the Mission District. Sly, Bubba, and a couple of other people that had some interest in doing gigs there. It was a hip little place, a hot little spot before the ethnic changeover in the Mission District in terms of it being a Hispanic community. Bo Peep's was a Black club in the sense that there was a lot of rhythm and blues there, but it was really a multi-ethnic thing. I don't know if Sly was ever in a total Black environment. Hamp was kind of Sly's buddy or whatever. He helped him with the gigs and I think we brought Sam & Dave, Howard Tate, and a few other people in. Rose was around, too. The band was hip and I don't think any of us expected more than what it was. There were these guys, as a matter of fact, we had to run them out of there. This Muslim guy, Tommy Manning, was a little poobah, but he had Sly in fear. He intimidated the hell out of Sly. Sly called me in and asked me to help him and I said, "With what?" He told me who the guys were and I said, "Let's go over there." We went over to his house and I told him that I was in the loop and cool out.

HAMP "BUBBA" BANKS: His mom didn't particularly cater to me because I was in a different league than her son. His sister Rose, little country girl sitting at the table looking at me, started liking me. I told him, "I think your sister likes me." He said he knew. "But I'm a dirty motherfucker," I told him. "I'm a pimp." I found out later from her that he did tell her that, but that didn't stop her. She became my woman. I had her taking tickets at the door. She could sing. If somebody didn't show, she took the stage and satisfied the crowd.

FREDDIE STEWART: There were times when I had my group Freddie and the Stone Souls, he'd be upstairs, listening, and we'd be rehearsing downstairs. He would call me and say, "Fred! Come up here, man." I had two horn players, a tenor and an alto, and he'd say, "Have the tenor player play the seventh," or something "and have the alto play the fifth, right in that part you had them doing," some particular horn line. "See how it sounds." I'd try it, and you know, it worked. He loved to do things like that.

LARRY GRAHAM: When my mother and I started working together, I was playing guitar and so it was guitar, my drummer from my band, and piano. And we worked like that for a little while, but then we went into this one club where they had the organ and I started playing the bass pedals and the guitar at the same time. So we had bottom. But when the organ broke down, we missed the bottom. I went and rented a bass, temporarily, until the organ could be repaired. I was not planning on being a bass player. As it turned out, the organ could not be repaired—there was no parts available or whatever.

My mother at that point had traveled all over the world—she sounded almost identical to Dinah Washington when she sang, and she played almost identical to Erroll Garner. So that was the combination. She did standards, jazz, blues, pop, country, whatever.

CYNTHIA ROBINSON: I went with Sly to this club where [Larry Graham] was playing with his mother, and I heard him playing. Sly said, "What do you think of this guy?" And I thought nothing special. But Syl always had another ear and another eye.

LARRY GRAHAM: Any club that you worked in, they have the people there that are your regulars. And you kind of see them there all the time, but you don't really know them. They just come to the club. When we started working at Relax with Yvonne's on Haight and Ashbury, there was a lady who was coming down to the club that was just into the music. And not necessarily a close friend of ours or anything. But by this time, I had developed this style. We didn't have a drummer now, so I would thump the strings to make up for not having a bass drum, and pluck the strings because I didn't have that snare drum backbeat. And I developed this style, but I didn't think I was developing anything new. It was just out of necessity. Just trying to do the gig right, make it sound good and feel good. After a while of doing this, that's just the way I play. I never thought about playing the overhand style, the way bass players were playing then, because I wasn't gonna be a bass player. So even though musicians would look at me like "that's a weird way of playing you are playing there," it didn't matter, because it just was not my instrument. I didn't care what anybody thinks, says, or nothing. At the same time, I'm not listening to bass players to be influenced by them, because I'm not a bass player. I'm a guitar player. In my brain, this is just a temporary gig.

Anyway, she used to come in the club all the time, but she was also a fan of Sly on the radio. Somehow, she found out that he was going to be starting a band. I don't know if he was talking about it on the radio, or how she found out, but she found out and took it upon herself to start calling the radio station and telling him, "There's this bass player you have to hear." And she was persistent enough to where finally she got him to come down and hear me play. When he heard me play, he approached me that night and was talking about the group.

I was aware of who he was. When he talked about me joining this band, I knew that he had some influence and popularity going to where this might be a good move, but I wasn't totally positive. So I talked to Mom about it extensively, because it would mean me leaving playing with her to join his band. Obviously, I couldn't be working six nights a week with her. Her thing was like, "Well, I've been all over the world, I've done it, and you go for it." Maybe she was more aware of the potential at that time than I was, but through her encouragement I said okay.

And bass players in those days—playing lead guitar and singing was kind of out front, where bass players were more in the background, which is cool if that's where you want to play. But I was never there in my thinking. I was out front singing, playing lead guitar and stuff. I think it was because of all that focus on the guitar, when it came to bass, there was nothing to interfere with creating this style that later on became different. When Sly heard this—by that time, I had developed it a lot—he asked me to join his band. Now I was going to be combining that style with drums. That in itself, looking back, was really something different. And he being the person he was, he was able to see that this is something that would be a contribution to the band.

JERRY MARTINI: When he used to do KSOL, I used to come down and sit around on the show. I was playing out with George and Teddy at the Tiger à Go Go at the Hilton. I stopped by the show and asked Sly to bring some pot. He got the engineer so high one time that he couldn't do the news. That is where we started hooking up again. He would talk to me over the microphone and I told him that he should sing his whole show. He had a piano behind him. He would sing the commercials. He did stuff that was so unique, his show on KSOL was so much hipper than his show later on KDIA. He was just a creative young disc jockey. He always gave the same weather report. In San Francisco, it was always sixty-nine degrees, year round. That is what he gave, whether it was ninety degrees or forty-seven degrees. He was so hip.

I would go to the radio station and tell him that we really have to start a band. "Being a disc jockey is a dead-end street because you are only going to get up so high. You have so much genius and so much talent and I want to play in your band." He thought that I was the funkiest White boy around on saxophone, and I was. It is not that there couldn't have been any other ones, there just wasn't. All of my peers were into Dave Brubeck. All the White people that I grew up with didn't like Black artists. I listened to the sax player for Little Richard, who was my favorite back then. That made the hair stand up on my arms. Sly loved the way I played. He used to come down to the Condor.

JOHNNY MORRIS: He would always get to the station late, about two or three minutes before his shift. He'd have one foot out the door before his shift was over. One night, he had a gig or something around ten-thirty in the evening and he was working until midnight. He asked me to come and bail him out and tell the program director that there was something wrong with the station. He signed the station off around ten o'clock. Check this out, I turn the radio on and he sings "The Star-Spangled Banner" on the air and then shuts the station off and splits. Like there was some technical difficulty. Until midnight. No, it was Sly. If you had a 40 percent share of the market, you couldn't do any wrong.

ALAN SCHULTZ: Because his career took off in '67, his appearance on the air was so inconsistent. We never knew when he was going to be there. The rest of the guys started to resent that—that Sly could fall in and out based on his schedule and their schedule would be disrupted because of it. He went over to KDIA in the latter part of '67.

JOHN TURK: What eventually happened is that we were late to rehearsal, once or twice, so the next time we were late for rehearsal, Sly put a sign on the door that said anybody can be replaced. Instead of firing us outright, he let us keep the gig at Little Bo Peep's and that is when he got Larry and Freddie and put that group together.

CYNTHIA ROBINSON: When Sly got the Stoners together, it was literally made up of Johnny Heartsman's old band. John Turk was his trumpet player and something happened with his lungs, so he started playing keyboards. And he was a disc jockey on the radio, until midnight or whenever he got off. We'd be playing there from nine o'clock to whenever he'd show up. Then we'd do whatever we'd worked on with him. But the saxophone player and the drummer used to drink about a gallon of Gallo wine every night, and by the time Syl would get there, they were toasted. I mean the eyes, one was looking this way, and the other eye was looking here. They'd be smoking onstage and leaning up against the wall.

Cynthia Robinson, 1968.

Freddie's group would come in, him and Gregg and Herb, who I couldn't stand. They'd come in and sit there and watch us, and they'd be out there talking, and they'd have these smirks on their faces and they were laughing, and other groups would come in and laugh at us, because they were playing the wrong changes. One night, I was taking a solo, I was really embarrassed, this blues song. I was literally crying, tears were rolling down my face because they were out there laughing at the group. And Syl had already asked us not to smoke on stage, not to drink on stage. They would do this while he was on the radio, and when he came in, they'd straighten up, like they was really cooking and act like they was really into it.

One day I just told him, "You know, I can't play with you anymore. Maybe later on, if you get something together, I'd really love to play with you. But I can't play with these guys any longer because I'm embarrassed. I'm used to playing with a group that takes more pride in the things that they do. They play the wrong changes. Other groups come in, musicians, entertainers, and they're laughing at us when you're not here. It doesn't matter to them, they don't care. So I just don't want to play." He said, "Come to my house tomorrow at three o'clock." And he turned around and walked off.

THREE

BOYS. GIRLS. BLACK. WHITE

Publicity shot, 1968.

CYNTHIA ROBINSON: I came to his house at 3:30 the next day, and I saw all these different people. He was talking about getting a group together that played all the music he wanted to do. He wanted to do originals. And he liked to take a song, like the first song we did as Sly and the Family Stone, Ray Charles's, "I Don't Need No Doctor." It's not a horn thing, but he rearranged it so the horns had these punching, funky lines. And the harmony was such that when we hit it was "Whoop!" It was screaming! And it shocked me because I had never played in a group that was that together. I had heard it on a record before, but I had never been a part of it. And when I hit that first note, I was like "Whaahh." I put my horn down and just listened. He said, "Play it, play it!" So I came in with the part, and I just knew, it felt so good.

You can come in either way, from the garage or the front door and down a very narrow passageway. You walk into the room, it looked like someone had used it as a storage place, but at that time it had just all been knocked out, so it was just space there, nothing elaborate, just space. My brother had a carpenter come in and turn some things around, and for a while he stayed there. Large enough for all the musicians to just sit in there comfortably, but nothing fancy. When you look out of the window, all you see is street. You're on the lower level, you see the lawn out in front of the house. It's right on the corner there. Sly had a place downstairs for himself. His mom and dad more or less had upstairs. He had his little waterbed in the back.

I was just excited because I knew we were going to do something great. I didn't know what. Primarily we were going to have some fun, because after listening to Larry play—very accomplished. You didn't have to tell him how this song goes, what the changes were. Jerry Martini knows more than he plays. So for me, all the musicians I was playing with were up there.

What we started out doing was Top Forty. But only, the whole idea wasn't to do Top Forty. The whole idea was to have our own group, to have our own sound, to have our own following, to have our own everything, to go out and make records. But we did it transitionally, just by doing the Top Forty, and every once in a while, we'd throw in one of our own songs. We did that until it took over.

GREGG ERRICO: The only person I really knew about was Jerry Martini, 'cause I had seen him play with George and Teddy. So I kind of knew Jerry, but I didn't know him. I had seen him around. And Larry, I had never heard of or seen. Freddie, I'd played with—Sly's brother played guitar and sang—we already had a relationship. Sly, I knew from the radio and the Stone Souls. Cynthia and Rose, I didn't know. There was a lot of family element involved. There was a lot of pre-relationships, like me and Freddie were already tight, playing together for a year, and Sly was known by everybody in the band, because he was the radio personality. Here was this guy who was a disc jockey and we're going to form a band and we're already excited. We're going to have some great opportunities.

LARRY GRAHAM: Jerry Martini already had done some other things for him. Al Lewis hired me as a lead guitar player for Al Lewis and The Modernistics. I would play all these lead guitar parts. He'd be out front with the guitar behind his head, scooping up and grinding, doing all this kind of stuff, and I'm back playing the guitar. Jerry Martini was in that band, so we had already worked together. But then that was with me as a guitar player. As time goes by, I emerged as a bass player. But we had worked together.

JERRY MARTINI: I was playing with George and Teddy at the time and that is why they didn't speak to me for years afterwards. Our next gig was for eight hundred dollars a man a week at Caesars Palace, which was incredible money. But I saw something in Sly and believed in him so much that I gave up my apartment, I moved in with my in-laws, and lost everything I had and went to work for ten dollars a night, what we made at the Winchester Cathedral. Married. Three kids. My mother wouldn't speak to me for two years. Everybody on my block in Mountain View thought I was completely nuts.

CYNTHIA ROBINSON: At the rehearsal, Freddie said, "How we going to do this, man?" because they were both guitar players. "You going to play guitar sometimes, and I'm going to play sometime? How we going to do this?" And Sly said, "No, you are the guitar player now." So Sly was like looking around because there were different instruments in the room, and there was this spinet organ. And he said, "I'll play this." Freddie said, "Okay, man," because he knew he could play a little keyboard. But when we started rehearsing, he sounded so pitiful on the keyboard.

FREDDIE STEWART: Right from the start, we began to do our own thing. Sly would come up with an idea for a song and he had it together, more or less. In fact, he played keyboard a little bit, but only really started playing keyboard because I didn't play keyboard. I played guitar. He played guitar before I did, but he said, "Freddie, you play guitar, I'll go to the keyboard." But he had a way of presenting the song and then letting us go. Larry ended up playing the bass unorthodox. I ended up playing a lot of guitar licks differently, only because when we started doing our own thing, it really was our own thing, and we threw all those other things out of the window.

CYNTHIA ROBINSON: After rehearsal was over, Larry says, "Okay, let's take a vote and see who will be the leader." And everybody turned and looked at each other and said, "What is he talking about?" It's obvious who the leader is because he went and handpicked everybody. And Syl, you could see he was thinking about just how he was going to say this—"There's not going to be any vote. This is my band, I'm the leader of it, and if you don't like that, there's the door. 'Cause there ain't gonna be no vote." There was no question to anyone in the band who the leader was. It was made very clear to us.

JERRY MARTINI: Absolutely, it was deliberate. He told me about it before we even started the band. He was so hip on that—he knew exactly what he was doing. He was so far ahead of his time. He intentionally had me in the band. He intentionally wanted a White drummer. There was a shit pot full of Black drummers that could kick Gregg's ass and there was a lot of Black saxophone players that could kick mine. He knew exactly what he was doing. Boys, girls, Black, White.

CYNTHIA ROBINSON: Syl just told us where he wanted us to shop—North Beach Leather. But he never told us what to wear. You could pick and choose out of that shop. Sly wore knickers, and at that point, it wasn't about colors. I wore stripes and polka dots. Larry had puffy sleeved shirts with tight pants. Later on it got to the point where we would wear the same colors but different outfits, as long as it was red, black, and white. But we'd all have different styles. And then some nights we'd wear the silver or the gold. We could pick and choose something, as long as the colors were consistent. The main thing, Sly said, was to dress just the way you feel comfortable, makes you feel good.

GREGG ERRICO: We would dress psychedelic—polka dots and colors and vests and fringe and leather booties that came up to your knees. It was wild. To look at us and to hear us, it was kind of like "What am I about to see? What am I about to hear? What's going on?" It was intense. I mean we stuck our asses out there on the line and we made it work somehow.

This was his concept. He had tried a couple of things musically that were just really ordinary. If you know Sly, you know that he thought big, he thought different, he thought unique. Whatever he was going to do had to reflect that. After the first couple of things when he tried to put a group together, I guess he realized that he was going to have to start from scratch and make it be unique from the get-go. He figured if he would start mixing all these unique elements, if he put the right combination of people together, he would end up with something that was going to be unique, just by nature, just by default.

Gregg Errico, 1968.

JERRY MARTINI: We bought clothes from secondhand stores and thought that was unique. Sly was an expert at that. Sly had some great-looking clothes. I remember we both bought these jackets that were like cavalry jackets. They were from the military, West Point stuff. Sly directed everything. He insisted that I put my hair back and spray it, that I grow the beard and dye it black. Sly left Larry alone on his style. He helped and made suggestions to Cynthia and myself. We also had band colors, which were red, white, and black. He hated uniforms. He was the first person that I met that was into a thematic thing. So we looked like a band, but everybody had on their own clothes, which was a lot hipper. He told me how to dress always. He told me how to do everything from day one because I was "Mister Nightclub," Top Forty look.

GREGG ERRICO: We rehearsed for six nights, rehearsed every night and we got our first gig, Winchester Cathedral. The guy who ran it, he was our first manager, Rich Romanello. Matter of fact, he was the one that got us the gig. It was a teen club down on in the peninsula on El Camino. Chocolate Watchband, I think, had played in there, and Strawberry Alarm Clock, those kind of groups. So we were from a whole 'nother world. But people liked it, and they would come. Then we started doing after-hours. We'd play the beginning of the night, we'd take a break, one-thirty, two, something like that. Then we'd start the after-hours set, and on the weekends everybody from all the clubs like on Broadway and in the East Bay would come down there. If Smokey Robinson was in town, everybody would show up. We developed this after-hours thing there and we got to be the talk of the town.

JERRY MARTINI: We did a thing called the jazz riffs that blew people's minds—an eight-minute song of all these different riffs that we linked together. It just went different directions, different movements, different times. It would go up one beat, chromatically. It was our warm-up thing. Every rehearsal we would add a new lick to it; it didn't have to be the same key or the same time. We memorized it as we went along, we never wrote out charts. He just told us our parts.

GREGG ERRICO: To start out, we'd put together what we'd call the jazz riffs. It was a string of about five or six little short pieces, together in a medley, with all these fast tempos and all these tricky things and showed everybody's musical ability. That was right off the top. Then we'd go into some Wilson Pickett stuff or some James Brown stuff, with our arrangements, and Sly, Freddie, and Larry would do these dances, break down in the middle of a song, do the hambone. I mean, people would go wild.

JERRY MARTINI: With Larry Graham, his biggest stuff because he sounded like Lou Rawls was "The Shadow of Your Smile," "Tobacco Road," and other Lou Rawls songs. Cynthia played "St. James Infirmary Blues"; that was her big song. Mine was "Shotgun," played it, didn't sing it. We all had our little things. We used to go on one at a time. I used to go out by myself and start and musicians came out one at a time. We did that for years.

MICKEY HART: It was an after-hours thing. They started at twelve, one o'clock, and they went to dawn. And how they entered was Errico comes up and lays down a beat, a real righteous, straight-ahead backbeat. Then each one of them would come up and do a thing. They had fur boots and things like that. They would walk through the audience, go up onstage, and start their groove. It took like ten minutes to form the band. All of sudden, there they were, cooking. The thing that I remember really well is that if they stopped the song, Errico immediately—within a second, maybe a half-second—went into the next groove really quietly while Sly talked over the top of it. The groove never stopped. You'd come out in the morning and you had come out of a ritualistic kind of a setting where the music never stopped. It was kind of a religious experience in a Vegas lounge setting.

CYNTHIA ROBINSON: Whenever it was time to add some new songs, we'd stay after the gig, at two a.m., and rehearse new songs for two or three hours, and then we'd go home. He'd introduce us to new songs, and then original ones. And that's where some of the trademarks of our songs came from, like the "boom booms." Sly missed his lines on a song. He forgot to sing his part, so he filled it in with some "boom booms." The next time it came around, Freddie would fall in and do it in harmony, and then Larry would fall in with his harmony part. The next group of songs that Syl wrote, he added those "boom booms" as part of the song.

LARRY GRAHAM: The thing that stands out in my mind about that particular club is, Freddie, he had this version of "Try a Little Tenderness" that he sang and it would just bring tears to your eyes. He'd just tear the house down. He'd start off just with his guitar. That is where he first started doing that version, maybe that's why it stands out in my mind. Man, when he played "Try a Little Tenderness" and sang that, you never heard nothing like that in your life. Another experience from the Winchester Cathedral is one night it was an extra-late show, an after-hours show, and we wore pajamas.

FREDDIE STEWART: If someone were to ask me where my favorite place was in those days, it would definitely be the Winchester Cathedral. The intensity, the desire to really do well, not just to have fun, but to really do well, because the people that would come to some of the after-hours joints, they would just come to have a good time. But when we played, they're quiet, they're listening. It's like from our heart to your heart, and you wanted to do great, man, you wanted to do great.

CYNTHIA ROBINSON: I think by the time Sly and the Family Stone had got together, I had left Richmond and got my first apartment of my own on Shattuck in Oakland. When we went to Winchester Cathedral, for me to get back, I'd get a ride to San Francisco, and I'd wait for the buses. Then I'd catch a bus over to Oakland, then I'd have to wait for the city buses to catch a ride back home. By the time I got there, it was daylight. When we first started, we weren't making enough money for me to keep my place on Shattuck Avenue, so I stayed with Rose awhile and Vet was staying with Rose. This was the first time my daughter Laura and I were ever separated. I asked her father to take her until we could get a place together. So I stayed with Rose, and then I would go and visit Laura on a bus that would take all day long to get to Richmond. I lived with Rose and I think Vet was pregnant at the time. I don't really know what happened, I think she got sick and fell out of the bed, and that's where all the problems started.

JERRY MARTINI: Gregg had a timing problem. Frosty [who went on to play with Lee Michaels] sat in with us at Losers in San Jose and just kicked Gregg's ass all over the stage. He blew all our minds; great drummer. Gregg was a baby, a real cocky little kid, and his timing was bad. But Larry really fixed that. Larry was solid.

GREGG ERRICO: Sly was going to use Frosty, at first. That was his intention. Jerry told me that it was either Frosty or myself. Jerry was pushing for me. Quite frankly, I'm not sure why, because Jerry and I hadn't played together.

We worked for about six months, we developed a following in the Bay Area. The Losers in San Jose was one club, Frenchy's in Hayward, Winchester Cathedral in Redwood City, and we played Broadway a few times. A lot of the obscure places there was two people, but we'd do the whole night with those two people there.

DAVID KAPRALIK: I started as a trainee, and after a period, became head of national promotion, and went up the ranks at Columbia, became head of A&R. I signed Streisand, Andy Williams. John Hammond was on my staff and he took me down to Folk City and signed Dylan. John brought me Aretha Franklin. I had left Columbia and started my own production, management, publishing entity. Started with Peaches & Herb and just about the time Peaches & Herb were happening, I get a call from Chuck Gregory, and he was, at that time, a promotion man out of San Francisco. He's excitedly telling me about this disc jockey that has started his own group. I flew out on the first flight smoking to San Francisco. Within a day or two of Chuck calling me, getting me all crazed about this new group, I'm there and go out to Redwood City to the Winchester Cathedral. I walk in, the place was jammed. I think it was an after-hours club. This group came on and I was electrified. That first night, I didn't hear any original material. I heard jukebox. There was a song out at the time called "What's That Got to Do With Me" and I heard an arrangement that totally blew my mind. I knew right there that I wanted to sign them.

Chuck, Sly, and I went to House of Pancakes after the set and got to know each other. I made it very clear to Sly that I wanted to sign him. He wasn't making any quick acceptance, though he knew who I was; by that time, I had a pretty well-established reputation in the industry. I stayed in San Francisco for about a week, hanging out with Sly in this jeep he had, going from San Francisco to Redwood City to the gigs, riding around town with Sly while he was doing errands of a nature that I am not sure of to this day, sitting with him while he was on the air. He was formidable—putting together this group, disc jockey. I knew of his reputation as a producer. He checked me out. Sly is a street person and I was brought up a middle-class Jewish prince. He was getting to know who I was, at another level, whether he could trust me or not, I would assume. I didn't have to give him my greatest hits, he knew about those. I guess I did a lot of philosophizing as I tend to do with my middle-class New York, humanistic, liberal agenda.

Sly said, "Yeah, I want to sign with you," on this first trip.

I had, from the get-go, a sense of certainty about him. There was no question that he was a tour de force, that he was an original synthesis that created an original gestalt. My enthusiasm reached an all-time peak. Then, down in the family basement in Daly City, the group was gathered and they signed. It was after I signed them I said to Syl, "I can help you accomplish your dreams and you will be a star, a star that you want to be. At that point that you are that star, you are going to have power, and at that point, I won't be able to help you—only you can decide what you are going to do with that power, either use it beneficently or despotically."

Clive [Davis] had brought me back as the head of Epic. I was already back with Peaches & Herb. I put them on the Date label after Clive had brought me back. Above the table, it was an understanding that Clive and I had, that I kept my groups, Peaches & Herb, The Spellbinders, and Sly. I signed Sly after I got back, and it was okay for me to do that. It wasn't my own label, it was CBS's label, an anomalous situation. Conflict of interest, yeah, but I didn't sense it was a conflict of interest.

FOUR

PUSSYCAT A GO-GO, THE ELECTRIC CIRCUS

Publicity shot, 1968.

GREGG ERRICO: Las Vegas, that was definitely a test for what we had originally conceived. This would test us on all levels—individually, musically, what we were doing as a group, the way we dressed, the way we presented ourselves. We went down there to try it out at the Pussycat a Go-Go. They liked it and gave us a three-month contract. We found the El Rancho [Motel] on the Strip, where we could cook. Getting out of town was the logical thing. Las Vegas was an international town. Took our families sometimes for a month at a time. By then, I was married. Everyone was getting married. Jerry was already married and had kids.

LARRY GRAHAM: We first came to town, we drove in looking the way we looked and everybody had these Thunderbirds. Sly had a purple Thunderbird with a paisley top. Freddie's was pink with a white top, and mine was turquoise with a paisley top. Sly's and Freddie's was a '57, mine was a '55. That's how we pulled into Vegas. Lots of folks would come to the shows and it wasn't long before we got real popular there. It was really wonderful, people gave us a lot of love. We had some great shows. Playing all those shows was great because the sound kept getting tighter and tighter—it wasn't about rehearsing, it was about playing once you knew the stuff.

CYNTHIA ROBINSON: A lot of people who came there to play would come see us. Like one time James Brown brought his whole entourage to see us. Nino Tempo came in and sat in on his alto. A lot of different entertainers that played Vegas came to hear us play.

JERRY MARTINI: Bobby Darin was one of our biggest fans. He came and saw us in Vegas and would bring in a bunch of people. He was absolutely mesmerized by our band, the uniqueness of our band, the way we sounded, the way we looked.

FREDDIE STEWART: I think we met the 5th Dimension up there at that time. They were very nice people, as a matter of fact. But it was just a gig. We had fun times. I remember every once in a while, we'd wear these wigs, and Larry and I would jump off the stage at the end of the set. When we got to this part where we're going to jump all the way off, my wig slid all the way to the side. We got bored, we went out and bought some guns. We'd go out in the desert and shoot them. Cheap little twenty-twos, after shooting six, seven times, the gun got so hot, I had to put it down.

GREGG ERRICO: By that time, we worked up to where most of the set was originals. At first, they didn't want the originals. They wanted James Brown, Sam & Dave, "Land of a Thousand Dances," whatever—so we had to do that. But when we did them, we did them with our arrangements just to keep the integrity and spirit, the thought of what we wanted to do. So as we worked the originals into our set, we were able to make the turning point and do the originals at clubs where people never heard them. We developed an incredible audience down there. All the musicians came down after their gigs. It got to be another scene.

CYNTHIA ROBINSON: At the time, I wasn't aware that I had a blood disorder. I just used to think everybody had more energy than I did. But when you're busy, you can do more than you can normally do. And Sly had it going on. We would play from nine to two in the morning, and then catch a flight to Los Angeles to record. They'd be putting on a guitar part, and the horns would be sleeping, or the drummer was sleeping in the studio. After we'd finish, we'd fly back to Vegas and get ready for the gig. My lips were sore. They were bright red and like they weren't there half the time, like they belonged on someone else's face. It built chops, though, and a tone quality.

JERRY MARTINI: We did the first album at CBS on Gower Street in Los Angeles. We were off on Mondays from the Pussycat a Go-Go. Every Monday we flew in and spent twenty-four hours in the studio. We did that first album live. There was only four tracks available; this was before eight-track. There were a lot of people on that album, like family members, people from the church, Little Sister—Tiny, Vet, and Mary. And Rose, also.

LARRY GRAHAM: We did a lot of recording in L.A. I remember "Let Me Hear It From You," waiting for my turn to sing. My turn came in the wee hours of the morning, which was great because the song was a ballad and I had my deepest voice then. I was laid out on the couch asleep. My turn now.

GREGG ERRICO: Sly had a girlfriend, Nita. He met her down there. This was Las Vegas 1967. Here comes this group—predominately Black, but there was a couple of White guys and some girls, too. Las Vegas was the epitome of everybody categorized, musically and how they're supposed to look. We come in there and break every rule that there was. Sly met this girl down there, I think was the owner's ex-girlfriend. She was a White girl. They didn't like that, not even a little bit. It got pretty hairy there. We ended up about a week later running out of Vegas with our equipment and our lives. Sly got into a verbal confrontation with the owner. He threatened Sly with a blackjack.

JERRY MARTINI: She was a little bitch. She was cute, but a spoiled little bitch. I liked her, though, but she was a real pretty, high-maintenance chick. She really loved Sly and he really loved her, too. They had a real fiery, feisty romance. She fell in love with Sly and became his girl. Back then, it was a big deal. The club owner asked her to leave because she was going with a Black man. He told Sly that he was going to have to get rid of her, he couldn't have that shit there. The owner was an ex-cop. Sly got up on stage and put his hands up and told the story to the people and blew the club owner's mind. He said, "We are going to pack up and leave because I can't have my woman here and we are being racially persecuted, so rather than do what they tell us, we are going to leave." Everybody that was at the club stood up and gave us a standing ovation. The next thing we know the owner pulled his gun out in the back room and put it on Sly's head. I remember being told that we had two hours to get out of town. I got my family—it was serious shit—and we had a caravan with a police escort out of Las Vegas.

CYNTHIA ROBINSON: Very scary. I knew Sly's girlfriend Nita was having trouble with someone in the club. I remember later she said, "He's trying to get me out of here." I said, "You don't have to go." And then Syl investigated this. He was off the stage and we were still playing. He came back up on the stage, played another bar, went "boop," and said, "Let's go." There was no explanation. Everybody grabbed their stuff and started walking. It had something to do with her and the club owner. I remember him being in the back room, and they threatened Sly, physically. Her family didn't like her being with a Black guy. And they were calling and saying they were going to come up and shoot up the place, and the club was trying to eliminate the reason for it all, and get her out of the club. Syl said, "She's not going anywhere because she's with me," and that turned into something else. So he said if she has to go, we're going too—"I'm taking my band with me." The next thing I know, we were driving back to Los Angeles. Freddie was falling asleep and I was shaking him. Fog so thick, I don't know how we made it. It was God's plan, because Freddie couldn't stay awake, and I couldn't stay awake to keep him awake.

JERRY MARTINI: That was it—no more Pussycat a Go-Go ever. It wasn't long after that we went to New York.

CYNTHIA ROBINSON: When we went to New York, that was the first time I had ever ridden on a plane. I missed the flight, so Sly stayed back so he could ride with me because he knew I would be afraid. Being an introvert, I didn't say much the whole trip, but inside I was raging with ideas and thoughts and emotions. But no one knew it. They took us to this hotel. It stunk before you even got in the front door. I saw Frank Zappa walking through the lobby with no shoes on, and the floor was sticky and black and nasty. The soles of your shoes stuck to it when you walked across it. But what could we do? Nobody had any money.

JERRY MARTINI: We were living at the Albert Hotel in Greenwich Village. Gregg and I were roommates and listened to the rats crawling along the wall—it was filthy and dirty, terrible. We heard people getting killed. It was a fucking nightmare. We stayed one or two days. Next thing I know is we heard Sly scream-ing and yelling so much that we were staying uptown at the Park Sheraton Hotel. The management hated us while we were there. We were these weird-looking hippies, Black and White, come up to this White hotel, right around the corner from The Scene [a club] at Forty-sixth and Eighth. We used to take the subway to work every night at the Electric Circus, which was a joke.

LARRY GRAHAM: We were playing at this club in the Village, the Electric Circus. We played there for a few months, stayed at the Sheraton Hotel. I remember that, 'cause I had a dog that some-body had given me as a gift. So me and the dog were sharing a hotel room. The Sheraton, you can imagine what a problem that was. He was an Underdog—he was a basset hound. That was his name, Underdog. He had the droopy face and the droopy ears. Perfect Underdog. And we played the Electric Circus, which was a very interesting place. Again, we had a great following.

DAVID KAPRALIK: Jerry Brandt had left William Morris and started the Electric Circus. That was the first de facto appearance of the group. That is when the magic really got engendered. Packed the place. Of course, it was the happening spot then. I don't know if Sly was the draw to pack the place or if the packed place was the draw itself. The response to him was thunderous.

JERRY MARTINI: The Electric Circus was a hip place, the hippest place in New York. It was actually right in the times. There was no place like it in New York, probably no place like it on earth. Even the Fillmore out here was backwards compared to that. Big place with all the black lights and there were actually circus acrobats. They had sword swallowers. They had people that ate glass. It was a freak show, and we were part of the freaks. Jerry Brandt owned it. He also had a place in Chicago. People freaked out on us. In New York, you just don't wear orange pants. Nobody talked or messed with me on the subway because I looked like I was from outer space. We all looked like we were from outer space.

FREDDIE STEWART: Now the Electric Circus—that's where we first got started after the record [August 1967]. I liked it because, again, there were people dancing. We had a crowd, it was intimate. We met new people there. We had some friends there. They put us up in the Albert Hotel, a rat-infested place. We refused to stay there. Cynthia found a rat running around her room. By her bathtub was a big hole in the wall.

CYNTHIA ROBINSON: Me and Freddie were together at the time. We were boyfriend and girlfriend. He was married and he had a little boy, so that's immoral, yes. I was just totally mesmerized by Freddie. And then the story that I got from him, that was probably true, but girls have a way of falling for the story. I don't think that it was intentionally to get you to fall for it. I do believe that it did exist in him. But we're just natural mothers—"Oh, he's so sad, I can make him happier than that"—and when you're young and foolish you just rationalize that it's okay, because the way it started out, wasn't all right in the first place. So Freddie and I got a room, and I think Jerry and Gregg got a room, and Sly and Nita had a room. KC was there. I don't know what happened with that. I just know we had a room. You didn't flaunt stuff in his face, but we did sleep in the same room. But there was always two beds, so you could always explain something. Like I said, you didn't flaunt things; I wasn't hugging all over Freddie, but yeah, [KC] knew something, because he's a very bright guy. We got some hot plates in our rooms. It took about three or four hours to cook a pot of rice, took another hour or so to cook up a couple cans of turkey noodle soup. Then we'd pour it over that, and that was a meal for us. We couldn't eat out. There was no money and you know New York. There were no fringe benefits here. And then they found the Gorham, but we stayed at the Park Sheraton for a long time. And that was nice because they had a little kitchenette, so you could fry chicken in there.

GREGG ERRICO: We did the same thing at the Electric Circus as we did at the Winchester Cathedral. But New York, the East Coast, is more intense. So we had the energy that we had at our shows, with the East Coast thing injected into it. That was wild. We were staying at the Gorham or the Sheraton. We'd get dressed up in our stage wear and all take the subway, which was an experience. Any time we did anything, it was a movie. As weird and as loud as we were, we stuck together. I guess that's why we made it through…. We'd walk into that place and you couldn't get from the entrance to the back. They would pack them into that place, and the energy was so incredible. Those were the kind of things that would drive us, keep us all going. Because it was a struggle. Each time we broke through a barrier, we had to fight for it because we were so left field, so different. All along the way, as things moved forward, we still would push the envelope—musically, lyrically. Just the whole look of the thing, we always had that edge, but keeping the fun also. And we also had something to say.

CLIVE DAVIS: The Electric Circus was a vivid memory because they were happening at that time. I had asked to have lunch with Sly. I remember him and David having lunch in my dining room and feeling hesitant, but still it was my place to ask him because he had such vivid costuming and that was a concern to me. Did he consider the fact that all the satin and platinum wigs could risk that he would not be taken seriously or being looked upon as having a cabaret impact, which would have been injurious to his credibility as a new pioneering musician? There is no question that he considered it. He understood that this was very different, people could say that this is not Vegas, and people could say that this was not the vanguard, 'cause it was full of all different colors, satins, and everything of that nature. But he knew very much where he was going. It was one of the very earliest lessons that when you are dealing with revolutionaries that you take the lead from them.

JERRY MARTINI: I used to hang out at The Scene and there was this adorable waitress, Candy. We ended up being friends and I told her that I was married, but she came up to my room. The second or third time that she came to my room, she looked at me and said that she wanted me to leave my wife. I got three kids and a wife. I said that I was lonely and she was my companion. She goes in the bathroom and dropped a whole bottle of Valium. She said if I wasn't going to do it, then she was going to die right here. I said, "No you ain't, you are going to die outside." I grabbed her by the shoulder and led her outside my room. She sat down outside the door and I called the management and said, "I'll be honest with ya, I had a groupie up here and she started acting crazy and took a whole bottle of Valium and I made her leave and she is sitting outside my door—can you come up and remove her?" So they came up and escorted her outside, called a cab, and sent her to the hospital to have her stomach pumped. I didn't know that and I worried and worried. The next night I went down to The Scene and she was working. She came up and said she was sorry and asked me if she could come over again. I said no.

CYNTHIA ROBINSON: Jerry and I were going across the street in New York and passed by a barbershop. We were on our way to the little store there, to get a few little things, because we had kitchenettes in the rooms. They messed with us—Jerry being White and me being Black, and we had crazy clothes on, according to them, all that combination. I don't remember what started it, who said what, but they started cursing us, pulled their straight razors out, and ran us down the street. I know we hadn't done anything. When we got back to the Gorham, we told Sly what had happened to us. He went and got the fellas. Because if you did something to us, you were going to apologize. It didn't matter if it was the White boy or the Black girl or the Black guy. Whatever it was, you were going to apologize. So he went back over there and I think it ended up in a physical confrontation. But when we walked by that barbershop—and we stayed there for three months at one time, and four months at the other—we were never bothered again.

JERRY MARTINI: The first three months, we were there by ourselves and it was very difficult on my marriage. It was rough and we didn't have very much money. I remember having a hot plate, eating soup. Tough times. But we were new and making impressions. It was hot. The whole band was exciting then. I was in music heaven because we were doing it. We were on our way up and we were unified. We were a real band. Those were the days that Sly was with Nita and I was with my first wife. We would ride around the park and we would go rowing in Central Park. We were struggling, but we were doing it and it was exciting.

FIVE

PLAYING TOILETS

"Dance to the Music" sheet music.

AL DEMARINO: I signed them to the William Morris Agency. We had a bumpy winter because Sly's first album had been out that fall and was very slow moving. It got a lot of critical acclaim, but we were receiving very little airplay. The first winter was very tough.

DAVID KAPRALIK: I did send them on the road, William Morris booked it for me, and they were playing toilets in the snow and the mud. KC went along to manage. I couldn't. I was in New York.

KC STEWART: All I did was travel with them. I didn't have nothing to do. They just wanted me to travel with them, had me as the "front runner." Anything happened, I'd go ahead of them. People in those days, well, even these days, don't care nothing about rock groups. But we didn't have any serious trouble or anything like that, 'cause if anything happened, they come and tell me and I'd go ahead of them. Sometimes they'd get smart on a plane, to waitresses or someone. They'd say the police will be waiting at such and such a place when we get off the plane, and I'd say, "Well, I'll go first." I didn't look like a rock group. I was always dressed up.

JERRY MARTIN: Daddy took the band in the station wagon and Sly and I were in this jam-packed, broke-down, piece-of-shit van that we drove. Sly and I were up front in the van, leading this little two-car caravan.

GREGG ERRICO: Sometimes we rented a bus. Sometimes it was a station wagon and a van would take the equipment. We would venture off from New York City into the Midwest and other areas. We took a wrong turn and ended up in Detroit at about two or three a.m., when the city had been taken over by the National Guard, and we end up in the ghetto somewhere looking for gas. We get pulled over by the National Guard. Here we are in a station wagon and a van. The van is full of equipment, and Sly and Nita, the White girl, are in it. By the time we get out of the car, we are surrounded by about half a dozen National Guard jeeps, maybe a dozen or two National Guardsmen, rifles drawn. Now Sly wasn't the kind of guy that would just sit quiet and let a scenario go by unchallenged. You can imagine, this isn't the kind of scenario you want to mess with too much. He did. We thought we were going to die that night. And the National Guard, they didn't know. For all they knew, we were from Venus and it got pretty hairy. Sly wouldn't let it go down funky. They started messing with us, and he'd talk back. But he was a master at communicating in any situation. He was really good at it, although he would push the envelope to the edge. He would take control of the situation.

JERRY MARTINI: Nita was with us during the Detroit riots. She was hiding in the van. We had the van and the station wagon and we were on the road and pulled off the Ohio Turnpike to get gas. We went down Grand River Drive and saw all these fucking troops. We were waving at them. Next thing you know they had their machine guns turned on us, and that scared the shit out of me. Sly almost got us killed. They had just killed a Black man there recently at a motel. They used Southern National Guard. I remember this guy, six-foot-four, grabbed me by the pants and picked me up with one hand. They were treating us like shit and Sly got real arrogant. I remember one guy said, "Tell that nigger down at the end to shut up or we will shoot his ass." I told Sly to be quiet. Daddy was there and he told Sly to be quiet.

DAVID KAPRALIK: The group was on the road playing toilets and Sly came into my office, truculent. The album had died and he wanted out of his contract, he wanted out of Epic. By this time, I was getting feedback about the album from other musicians who were quite taken with it—Mose Allison, Tony Bennett. Teo Macero [jazz composer and Miles Davis producer] was telling me that his artists were telling him about the album. I remember saying to Sly that the response was great from other musicians, but it is not in the pop idiom. I said that he should do a record that pop ears can relate to and in between stick in your innovative schtick. He continued to be surly and said that he was going back to San Francisco.

CYNTHIA ROBINSON: The first album, Rose wasn't there. She finally agreed to it. Before that, she didn't want to leave her secure job, a record store, Sherman and Clay. Syl kept trying to get her and she would come over and listen, but she would be gone before we were done. Once she came down while we were blasting away and she asked, "Who's that down there?" She came down and listened and that turned her around.

JERRY MARTINI: I remember Sly and I going over to CBS Records and the executives saying to us, "This is what you should listen to." They gave us some shit and Sly threw it down and he looked at me and said, "Okay, I'll give them something." And that is when he took off with his formula style. He hated it. He just did it to sell records. The whole album was called *Dance to the Music*, dance to the medley, dance to the shmedley. It was so unhip to us. The beats were glorified Motown beats. We had been doing something different, but these beats weren't going over. So we did the formula thing. The rest is history and he continued his formula style.

Rose Stone, 1968.

DAVID KAPRALIK: Time passed and I didn't hear from him. Some months later, I get a call from him and he says that they were in the studio and he wanted to send me the record. So I got a demo of "Dance to the Music." It was that pattern, a repetitive theme interspersed with schtick. The original version that came from him was a little different. The intro was different and they took that "dance to the music" that Cynthia does from the middle and made it the intro. Originally, it didn't have that intro. It was a good edit. It went out and Lucky Cordell at WVON in Chicago broke the record. Not long, maybe eight months, once the group really took off, then I left Epic.

JERRY MARTINI: On "Dance to the Music," one of the sub-hooks was my clarinet. We used it on the medley. It was snowing in New York, and if we wanted to get paid by the union, which was so strong, you had to bring an instrument to the session. If a union guy came in, you better have your horn. I was freezing and just wanted to carry my small clarinet. I had already done my horn parts. I was in the back room, just fucking around with the tune. Sly walked by the studio and called me over. So then, on a lot of things, I used clarinet. That is how hits happen. He was smart. He heard something unique and it was the sound of a clarinet. When is the last time you heard of somebody in rock using a clarinet? I used to take my clarinet on the road for a long time until we got too fucked up, then I just played the lick on my sax. A lot of people thought that it was a soprano sax on that, but it was B-flat clarinet.

AL DEMARINO: We did some college work, we did some club dates, but it wasn't easy at that time because the airplay was slow in coming initially. Lo and behold, we struggled through the winter, then comes February and March of '68. "Dance to the Music" became a smash and what had been a struggle for a few months became a wide-open gate. We finished the spring semester at the colleges. Then we started doing the ballrooms. There was a wonderful circuit of music rooms in those days and we called them ballrooms—the Fillmore East, the Electric Ballroom, the Boston Tea Party in Boston, the Aragon Ballroom in Chicago, Grande Ballroom in Detroit, and Winterland and Fillmore and a few venues in L.A.

STEPHANI OWENS: I was working at Capitol Records for Dave Cavanaugh, longtime producer of Nat King Cole, Peggy Lee, Tennessee Ernie Ford. I got a phone call one day from Dave Kapralik asking me if I would be interested in working for Sly and the Family Stone. He said that they were looking for somebody to go on the road and to take care of administrative functions and asked if I would be interested. I never really spent any time with Sly. I had met him on different occasions in San Francisco and I was very curious what my role would be and what the expectations were. They booked me on a flight to New York. Sly met me at the airport with a dog, a pit bull named Max, a little puppy that he had just gotten the day before. They made accommodations where everybody was staying at the Gorham Hotel in New York and this ended up being our residence for six months.

JERRY MARTINI: Cocaine started to be in the scene before we moved to New York. I remember the first time that he gave it to me, first time I ever had it. I remember meeting God at his house at 700 Urbano Street in San Francisco in 1967. But he wasn't really into it then. It wasn't a big deal. It was, "Oh yeah, here it is." It was a big deal when we moved to New York.

STEPHANI OWENS: The day that I got to New York, Sly was there at the airport and we went back to the hotel and sat in the living room and went over what was expected of me. He said that he had a dentist's appointment the next day. He said that we would get back together when he got back from the dentist. He wanted to do some recording. It was in the middle of the week and we were getting ready to get on the bus and do some gigs for the weekend. He came back from the dentist's the next day. He came to my room. We're sitting in the living room and he puts a couple of bags of white powder on the table. That was my introduction to drugs. I had known about marijuana and had tried it. It gave me a headache and I didn't like it. I had heard about cocaine but had never seen it or knew anybody that did it.

So he puts this bag down and I ask, What is that? He says that it's cocaine, pharmaceutical cocaine. I said I thought you went to the dentist and he said he did. As it turns out, he was getting his drugs from the dentist's, which was amazing to me. Then I found out there was a doctor in New York that would give him and anybody in the group prescription drugs; yellowjackets [downers], etc. At one point, anybody that wanted drugs could go to this dentist and pay him whatever it cost for a visit and he would write a prescription, then go across the street and fill it. It got to the point that I could go myself, get prescriptions for everybody, go across the street to the pharmacy, get them filled, and come back with just bottles and bottles of pills.

JERRY MARTINI: We were on a little bus tour and my wife went to Boston to get a room ahead of time so we would have our room. We pulled into town and at this time they would allow straight-looking Blacks in some hotels, but no long hairs or hippie-looking people at all. We got there and I had my hair tied back, but I had a real scruffy looking beard. I walked by the lobby and they were all staring at me. I walked to my room, didn't even get unpacked yet—me, my wife, and three babies. I got a phone call from the desk and they said that I would have to leave because they didn't allow people that looked like me in their hotel. They suggested that I not even stay in town. It blew my mind. We left because they would have had us removed. We tried other hotels, nobody would let us in. We ended up staying in Cambridge because it was by Harvard and a lot of people had long hair there.

AL DEMARINO: In the early days of the Fillmore East, the norm was a three-act bill. I had Sly and the Family Stone come into the Fillmore East as the only other act but the headliner. There was no opening act. We had 100 percent special guest star billing below the great Jimi Hendrix Experience and that was Sly's first experience at the Fillmore East—strictly Sly and the Family Stone and the Jimi Hendrix Experience. It was four shows that were spoken of for countless months afterwards because Sly drove that audience insane. He was working the Hammond B-3 organ in those days, stage center, and midway through that show, the audience was absolutely insane. Of course, as great as Jimi Hendrix was, much of that crowd was there to see Hendrix. Jimi was the headliner. But Sly marched the audience out on a couple of those shows, literally, marched a good part of that audience out from the audience and into the streets. There had to be a lengthy intermission to bring that crowd down, although most of them were there to see the Jimi Hendrix Experience.

CYNTHIA ROBINSON: The fellows started doing the hambone. So Syl put the bass on me. He started playing something. I could do it for a while, but being that I didn't play bass, my fingers got tired and it was hard to lift them. So it was me and

Gregg keeping the rhythm going and Larry, Freddie, and Sly did the hambone thing. They jumped off the stage and went down the aisle and the crowd was going wild. They went down the side and went out the door. The whole place ended up getting out of their seats and following them out the exit and around the front and through the entrance and back to their seats. Amazing. By the time they got back, I was glad, 'cause I was fumbling like crazy My fingers felt like they had hundred-pound weights on them. But they got back up on stage and grabbed their instruments and we just blew the rest of that song and the people went wild.

DAVID KAPRALIK: A turning point was their first appearance at the Fillmore East, when it all began to change. Up to that point, each individual member had their star piece. Each member did a solo. At the Fillmore, he decided that it was going to be a one-man show and everybody else was going to back him up, and he took away all their solos. That was the first change of substance that I saw. Even though I had excellent relations with all the members, I believe my point of reference was always Sly. It was with Sly that I had my dialogue with, I didn't have one-on-one conversations with band members. He discouraged my doing it. He discouraged them having dialogue with me, I sensed. I never heard that, but that was my sense and I went along with it. I was busy and I didn't want to be divisive with the group and it worked for me to have my dialogue with Sly. We had a very intense dialogue. We spent endless hours together, roaming and ranging, musical to metaphysical.

JERRY MARTINI: I remember the night that Freddie first did cocaine; it was at the Fillmore East backstage and he changed from that day. It was real interesting to watch the personalities change.

DAVID KAPRALIK: Sly was my fifty-fifty partner in Daedalus and subsequently in Stone Flower Productions. This was an entity that I had and brought him into as a partner fifty-fifty. The first records were produced under Daedalus. Whatever percentage we got from production, Sly got 50 percent, I got 50 percent. The group got their performer's royalties. Daly City Music published Sly's music and that was fifty-fifty, Sly and myself. Sly and I were not partners in the management. Barbara Bacchus was my secretary in New York. She was my right arm. She implemented my decisions. She was a tasteful woman.

JERRY MARTINI: Barbara Bacchus was Dave Kapralik's partner. She was a bull dyke and I remember that she was pissed off at me because one of her girlfriends had the hots for me—she was bisexual. She was a real ballsy, hard-working production woman, real New York. She ran Daedalus Productions for Dave. They managed Peaches & Herb. Peaches & Herb supported Sly and the Family Stone. If it wasn't for Peaches & Herb, there may not be Sly and the Family Stone, because their royalties financed our operations.

CYNTHIA ROBINSON: The management company hired a woman named Barbara Bacchus to groom us. She wanted me and Rose to wear gowns. But I told her, "I can't do that. I'm just not a gown person, I just don't feel comfortable in one, and I'm just not going to do it." Rose took me to a store and bought me some false eyelashes that cost sixty dollars, which I still have. Rose tried to show me how to put them on, and I tried a couple of times, and I said, "No more, no more." So Syl went back and told them, "She doesn't want to wear gowns, then she doesn't have to wear gowns."

STEPHANI OWENS: We already had Stoner, the Great Dane that lived at Mama and KC's house in San Francisco. He was the dog that was around forever. But Sly got Max and then all of a sudden everybody got into dogs. So part of my job, while we were on the road on the bus, every stop we made, I would go to a bookstore and get dog books. I put in a subscription for *Dog World*, so that I could find out about these different dogs. I wanted to find out about Max, the background of the bulldog. Sly really got into dogs, and because he got into dogs, everybody else got into dogs. They each had one. It was just something that escalated. On the road, we had all these connections to breeders because we were going to those kinds of places. The *Dog World* book gave me more information about dogs and where to get dogs and they started going through the book—we had a lot of time to spend on this bus. All of a sudden the group decided they wanted to start ordering up all these dogs. Which ended up being one of my functions, to deal with these breeders.

JERRY MARTINI: We were dog experts. We got into the dog thing out of boredom on the road. It didn't start off with us buying the dogs, it started with the dog books. Everybody had their own dog encyclopedia. We would read the description in the encyclopedia and then everybody would know what the dog was. We would try and guess. It was like a game. Then we got out of that and chose our dog, we had exotic dogs. Larry had a Beauvais, a French fighting dog. Freddie had Giant Schnauzers and an Irish Wolfhound. Cynthia had a Rottweiler. I had, in the beginning, a Great Pyrenees and ended up with all the gentle giant breeds.

Jerry Martini, "Stand" session, 1969.

AL DEMARINO: What I started to do in '68 was concentrate on the festival dates for Sly. For example, we would do the normal one-nighters and ballrooms and do whatever college dates were available. Sly was quickly becoming a popular college act. We were doing, on average, during the school year, spring and fall semester, at our volition, up to four dates a week, which was exceptional at that time. Well-rounded dates and great money at the colleges, and this also helped bolster the popularity of the band. We were now getting festival recognition. We were getting the good college stages. We were getting good airplay.

> From *Rolling Stone*, October 26, 1968: "Sly and the Family Stone ran into trouble, in the form of a bust for possession of cannabis, as soon as they touched down in London Airport. It was all down from there on. After a week of hassles with promoters, the BBC and the press, their British tour was called off."

JERRY MARTINI: Everybody in the business knows that Larry Graham got busted for pot in London and that ruined our tour of England. It was a wrench in the whole thing and I felt very guilty about that for many years, except for the fact that I had enough sense to not take that shit across the border. They searched Larry and he had some pot on him and it fucked up the whole thing. It was a big mistake. I gave it to him. I was going to throw it in the toilet and Larry said no. So he took it and put it in his pocket. No way I was going to go across the border with that tiny joint on me. He said give it to me. Larry got in trouble for it because they caught him. We all got high, we all smoked pot then. Don't try and take it across customs; they were gunning for us. He made a mistake. I made a mistake. There you go.

AL DEMARINO: Our first time to Great Britain was September 1968, and that was supposed to be promotion and we were supposed to do a couple of ballroom dates. We went to do the ballroom dates, myself and my associate over in London at William Morris. Don Arden was the promoter. Sly was very particular in those days. Before he started using the Farfisa onstage, there had to be a Hammond B-3 organ there and it had to be in top-notch condition. Maybe the show should have gone on, who knows? But the fact is that there were four keys busted on the Hammond B-3 organ. It was a sold-out ballroom and it was one of the few dates that we were supposed to do in London. Everything else was press promotion. I must say that the band was threatened that night by some of Don Arden's people and there was tremendous tension backstage. Sly was basically told that he was going to go on, like it or not, and we chose not to. Sly had the guts to go out, grab the microphone, and announce to the audience in London why they were not going to perform that night. He started rapping with different people in the audience, and he literally, by his own presence and professional wherewithal, cooled down what could have been a very nasty situation.

DAVID KAPRALIK: William Morris had booked a tour of England for them with a guy by the name of Don Arden, who was a sleazeball. I had gone over there and met these three English guys, right out of Charles Dickens with their little record shop, and they were very much into rhythm and blues, American jazz. I had gotten them to do promotional advance work and the first venue they were booked into was sold-out, jam-packed with people. The group's instruments were delayed in transit. Sly refused to go on. That was the first time that I saw an adamance in Sly. Sly refused to use rented equipment. Things began to disintegrate more after that. My stress level went to its max to get them to perform. They went up there and did one or two numbers a cappella.

STEPHEN PALEY: I was photographing Sly in San Francisco. Sly and I got into his car and he didn't have his driver's license, so he used Freddie's. I said, "That isn't going to work if they stop you." He said, "They don't know the difference—we look the same." So he took Freddie's driver's license. We drove into San Francisco and went to a discotheque called the Rickshaw. Sly knew the disc jockey there and he brought an acetate of "Stand!" and gave it to the disc jockey to play. He watched the audience's reaction to the song and realized that there was something missing. The next day, he went back into the studio. He didn't use his own band, he used studio players. The band wasn't available, and what he needed anybody could do—I think Jerry was on the session—and they rerecorded that funky extension, after the fact, and edited it onto the record. "Stand!" was almost ready to go as a single, but he decided that it needed something more and he added that funky extension. It turned out to be a great record.

GREGG ERRICO: That was an overdub on that, that he put in. I remember doing the overdub on the high-hat; it was sixteenth notes. It had to be perfect. He would always go into this thing—it was fifteen seconds of it, then it fades out. He would open this door to this wonderful thing and then he would just take it away, wouldn't even go there. People would always ask, "Why didn't you just go there and let that be the song?"

STEPHEN PALEY: He was so together, he even wrote out the parts on music paper for the horn players, like a regular session, like a recording date. There were like old men horn players in there working with Sly. During the "Stand!" session, he even passed out W-4 forms to the players. He was that together. He was very businesslike. He took his music very seriously then, more serious back then. I remember he had a music theory book by Walter Piston, about orchestration, and he would always refer to it. You don't think of him as a great craftsman, but he was. He really knew his music stuff. He went to college, I think junior college; he wasn't stupid. He was very sophisticated musically, his chord structure and the progressions that he chose.

GREGG ERRICO: We'd cut the tracks and I would come in, very last thing, and do the drums over because the feel and even the range would be completely different. I'd lay the drums down to the new feel on the original thing that we cut. I would come in after everything was down, the horns, background vocals, everything, and put the headphones on, listen to the track, and cut new drums to that track. I remember sessions at Pacific High in San Francisco, a couple of blocks from the Fillmore West, cutting "Sex Machine."

JERRY MARTINI: At the end of "Sex Machine," when Gregg was playing his drum solo at the end of it, there is laughing. That's because we were all standing behind Gregg, making fun of him. He looked around and saw everybody and they all started laughing.

AL DEMARINO: The first time Sly did *The Ed Sullivan Show*, he absolutely went off from the stage and into the audience which, at that point, had never been done by a musical or a variety entertainer. He deliberately left the stage and went into the audience, which had never been done. The audience was enraptured and inspired by it.

JERRY MARTINI: It was our first live television show in front of twenty million people and it was real positive for Sly because he was so on, so ahead of his time. They didn't tell us until the last minute that we had only so much time, so we reorganized our songs and our dance—we had dance steps back then. We had a show. This was before people used to bring their tracks and panto-mime to their tracks. We were probably the first band to record a track and then sing live to it.

STEVE TOPLEY: I was working for Stone Flower Productions, not independent. We were way ahead of the time. I got the thing started on "Hot Fun in the Summertime." Epic didn't want to put the record out because it was already getting into August. I'm sitting with Sylvester in the house in San Francisco and I'm play-ing the acetate and Sylvester looks at me and says, "You believe in it, don't you?" I say, "Syl, we gotta put it out now." I pressed up acetates and took it out on the road. I got into Minneapolis and the Columbia branch manager goes, "You're outta your mind." I got the acetates on the air and forced it out. The station that broke "Hot Fun" was CKLW in Detroit, number one station, Top 40. It was Top 40 radio that broke Sly, not what they call R&B. Sly wasn't anything on FM. Not too much R&B—they played it because, hey, he's our brother.

From *New York Times*, July 7, 1969: "The Newport Jazz Festival was invaded last night by several hundred young people who broke down a section of the ten-foot fence surrounding Festival Field and engaged in a rock-throwing battle with security guards. When the main gates were opened to prevent further assaults on the fence, they swarmed down through the 21,000 spectators, leaping over chairs and railings. As they rushed toward the stage where Sly and the Family Stone, a rock group, was playing, they drove paying customers from their seats, occupied the boxes at the front of the field, and filled a pit in front of the bandstand intended for photographers."

JERRY MARTINI: Sly's effect on large audiences was amazing. At Woodstock, everybody was in their sleeping bags and he got everybody up out of their sleeping bags. Sly had this Napoleonic or Hitler-type control when he was on. He could make them riot. He could make them sit down. Make them do anything when he had the power. We were the reason that the Newport Jazz Festival was closed down. When we were there, there was thirty thousand kids outside because the place was too full to let them in. When we came on, we came out with our usual high-energy effect and the kids were jumping up and down. During the song "You Can Make It If You Try," they crashed the fence. They did it with such force that they trashed our bus with all our stuff on it. We had to take cabs back to New York City because our bus was trashed. I eventually got my saxophone case back. A lot of my belongings were on that bus. It was like a riot. They came in and caused a lot of disorder. We couldn't control it and that is when they stopped the festivals for a long time at Newport, not because of us, but because of what happened. I know we got blamed for it.

DAVID KAPRALIK: [Newport producer] George Wein shit a brick. Crowds pushing down his fences to get to Sly. People standing up on seats. It drove him crazy. Sly created an enormous sensation, people pushing to get closer, people moving. Again, it was hysteria that Sly generated.

AL DEMARINO: George Wein was beginning to lose audience and he obviously realized the tremendous appeal of the rock and roll acts, Sly being a great example. It was an incredible performance. The band gave one of their most dynamic performances ever that particular night. A drizzle ensued, a steady drizzle, and the audience got so carried away that they were jumping up and down in the mud and they were beginning to rush the stage. George Wein was petrified that there was going to be an incredible riot and he literally called for reinforcement. The cops from Newport turned out with masks and shields. Sly had decided to take them to such a peak where I am sure that they had never been. It reached a point that George came up to me backstage and said, "You have got to have him bring this crowd down, there is going to be a riot."

I looked behind the stage and I saw patrol cars pull up and the cops with heavy plastic masks and shields. They were intending to charge the crowd because they thought the crowd, I guess, was going to tear the stage apart and march into the town. That was the craze that Sly had this crowd in. It got so frightening that one of the senior William Morris executives there with his wife came up to me and said, "Look, we have to run, we have got to leave here with our lives, there is going to be a riot." He took my wife and his wife and left. I didn't realize it until it was over and they were gone.

AL DEMARINO: Sly had doubts about playing the Apollo. We had already done a benefit concert in Harlem late summer '68, prior to these dates, outdoors, in the park. We knew we were getting the Black airplay. Obviously, Sly's records were selling to Blacks, too. There was a marketplace out there and Sly and the band relished that. They didn't see themselves as strictly a rock band. Point being, when we did the Apollo, there was some doubt about doing it. The Apollo was still the showcase for the Black marketplace at that point. We put Redd Foxx to co-headline, with Sly and the Family Stone closing. At those four shows, I think Sly was late for maybe three of the four dates. Redd Foxx improvised. He would be sticking his arm behind the curtain to try and feel the equipment to see if Sly was set up yet, talking about doing long shows for short money. Four shows. The audiences went home a little later than normal, but they had an incredible time.

GREGG ERRICO: I remember us being at the Apollo and thinking that this is the place that if you don't get down in the first fifteen seconds, you're out of there, they throw shit at you. Being in Harlem and being a White boy playing drums, I felt pressure. I remembered the gig at Central Park, way up on the Harlem side. The audience was all Black, and it wasn't a particularly great concert. We were sick. Sly was sick. I had the flu. We went up and did it and it was a tough audience because they were checking us out. Probably most of those people had never seen us. Everybody had come to see what this was all about, this guy out of San Francisco who had a group that was White, Black, and had females. It was a check-out session.

JERRY MARTINI: I used to go out by myself and start. The other musicians came out one at a time. We did that for years. We even were doing that when we played at the Apollo Theater the first time. When Gregg was out there he stood in the back, he is full-blooded Italian—he looks like he could be mixed. But when I came out there with my white skin and long hair, there was silence and boos. Sly came out and stopped the concert and said that, true, they had White people in the band, but Jerry can play the saxophone. I had to play by myself. My stomach was shaking and I thought that I was going to pee my pants. A woman's voice: "All right, send him out here." The guys started laughing. Sly kicked off a song. Happiness everywhere. From that point on, whenever we played a show at the Apollo, I was accepted. That was one of the highlights of my life.

SIX

AS BIG AS LIFE

Woodstock film still.

LARRY GRAHAM: Woodstock was a big concert that we were going to play that had a lot of artists. I had no idea that it was going to be as big as it was. Getting to the concert, I realized that there were a lot of people, but still not how many until we played. Our songs would segue one into the other and many times there wasn't a place where you could get a big audience response. When we did stop playing, there was this tremendous roar unlike anything we had ever heard. It was dark and you couldn't see all those people, but to hear that was like, Wow! To go back out and play the encore after hearing that, it made us rise to a level we had never been musically There was so much energy, everybody reached deep down inside and pulled out some stuff we didn't know was there. From that point on, once you tap into a certain zone, you know you can go back there because you have now tasted that. The audience might not be as big as Woodstock, but to play anything after that, you know you have capabilities beyond. So that took our concerts up to a whole 'nother giant notch, to where the concerts became an experience, for the audience and for us. We started playing in this new zone we had never played in before and it was some of heaviest stuff I had ever been involved in. That is what I felt Woodstock did for us.

JERRY MARTINI: We thought that it was going to be a regular festival. We had no idea that it was going to be that big. We were staying in a little motel. We didn't play till the second night. We went over there and walked around in the mud. They didn't fly us in in helicopters; they were being used for Medivac. They drove us in through the maze in a couple of limousines and treated us like royalty. We were supposed to start at ten o'clock. We sat around in tents and didn't go on until three-thirty in the morning. Everybody was asleep in their sleeping bags. We were a little bit bummed, but people got up out of their sleeping bags. Everything was so late, we got onstage and just kicked ass.

GREGG ERRICO: We were scared. I've heard the other acts that were on it say the same thing; you look out there, butterflies. Before you even looked at the audience, you could feel the energy there and you knew it was intense. We were supposed to go on at eight o'clock. We were in the trailer, our adrenaline up, ready to go. [Woodstock producer] Mike Lang kept coming in. Things were running behind, he said, hang in there. Two hours went by. We didn't go on till three-thirty. We were physically tired, just from all the adrenaline going through your body, peaking and coming down again, getting fired up to go on, for six or seven hours.

We went on and you could feel the weight of it. It was heavy. This was the second day, the middle. People were sleeping, it was the middle of the night. It had just rained. Just the experience of getting there for the audience was a major no-one-had-planned thing. They had already been there for twenty-four, maybe thirty-six hours, hearing music, having to find food, standing in line to go to the bathroom. They were spent. It was nighttime. You had been waiting to do your thing for hours now. They were in their sleeping bags, tired, burnt out, hungry, who knows what, asleep, and you went on the stage to make these people get up and going. You could feel it. We started out and did the best we could. You could feel it drag and then, all of a sudden, the third song, I think, you started seeing heads bop up, people starting responding a little bit. Sly could feel it. He had it down by this time. He was great at working an audience in any situation, any diverse situation. He started talking to them. You could feel everybody start to listen to the music, wake up, get up, start dancing. Halfway through the show, the place was rocking. Really incredible experience.

> From *Rolling Stone*, September 20, 1969: "As the
> night wore on, it was Battle of the Bands; Grateful
> Dead, strained after Canned Heat, climbed out

onto a limb without hopes that the audience would reach up to them; it didn't. Creedence Clearwater, clear and tight; a static Janis Joplin, cavorting with Snooty Flowers, her backup band just that; Sly and the Family Stone, apart in their grandeur, won the battle, carrying to their own majestically freaked-out stratosphere."

GREGG ERRICO: We got a lot of recognition after Woodstock. The band stood out. We increased our audience vastly from that performance and the exposure that it gave the band. To me, the bigger our audiences got, the more intense things got. There was no middle ground; it was going to be intense, no matter if it was going to be intense to the positive or intense to the negative. It depended on how Sly would handle it. On one hand, he had the capabilities of handling all that attention, fame, big audiences. But on the other hand, there was another part of him that didn't want it, couldn't handle it, and wanted to be away from it. This fight always went on, where he wanted to be the biggest, the baddest, best, and then, when he got it, he didn't want to be it; he was scared of it.

STEPHANI OWENS: I really think that he was happy in a small room playing his music. But when it came time for him to get on stage in front of a crowd, the thought of it was fearful to him. Once he got onstage, it was a whole other story, because he was the kind of person that wanted to take on accolades and feel that energy.

GREGG ERRICO: We played Harvard Stadium with Wilson Pickett. He was the headliner. Wilson Pickett is someone we really respected and we did some of his songs. The band felt that this was an important gig and we felt that we had to go up there and kick some butt and take our space. Pickett took some cocky position. There may have been flack about when the band was going to play, I don't know. But something went down with his management. A bad attitude that prevailed. We went up and did our thing.

KITSAUN KING: My sister met Sly while she was just walking down the street in our neighborhood. He lived in our neighborhood on Urbano. He was just driving down the street and saw her and started talking. That is really how it began. Next thing you know, she was taking off with him and going to Woodstock. He wasn't really into heavy drugs then. When Deb and I met Sly, he was a different man than he was soon to become. Granted, there wasn't a long space between what we met and what he turned into, but there was a space. The man we met was not the man that we ended up knowing two years later. Shortly after Woodstock is when he moved to L.A.

JERRY MARTINI: There is a cloud flying over Sly from the time he moved down to Los Angeles. Things really changed when he moved there. That's when Gun the dog and all the fucking assholes came into his life. Feels nice saying that, too. It was havoc. It was very gangsterish, dangerous. The vibes were very dark at that point. There was a cloud flying over that place.

STEPHANI OWENS: At a certain point after we did all this riding around on the bus, Sly decided that he did not want his base to be New York. So he started Stone Flower Productions in Los Angeles. The office was set up on Vine Street, right across the street from Capitol Records. Dave lived around the corner. We set Los Angeles as the base and started recording out of there. One of my jobs was to find housing for everybody. First, we lived in an apartment off Apcar, near Griffith Park, above Hollywood and Vine. Then we found the house in Coldwater Canyon.

It was an old house. Lots of people. This was after we came off the road and ordered up all these dogs. He had Max, the English bulldog. He had a pit bull, and we brought Stoner down from San Francisco. Stoner and Max were staying with me when Sly had his first apartment. When he moved into Coldwater, I moved into that house for a little while. There was this other dog that he had that was a Schipperke called Shadow, a little small black dog with no tail. I kept Shadow and Stoner with me and he took Max to Coldwater, and he had this other dog, a pit bull, who was evil and mean and bit people. Sly loved the dogs, but he was never a care provider of the dogs.

JERRY MARTINI: Coldwater had a lot of dogs. There was dog shit everywhere.

STEPHANI OWENS: He had a caretaker, Louis. Sly and Louis were basically the only ones who lived there. Debbie lived there part of the time, when she was with him. I always had another place, but I would stay there a lot. Everybody lived there at some time. Freddie lived there for a while, not the rest of the group. Loretta stayed there. They were like in and out. It was a very transient environment. I could show up any day and be surprised at who was there. Anybody that came could spend the night, and anybody, if they didn't have a place to go to, could stay there for weeks. There were that many rooms in the house.

GREGG ERRICO: Coldwater was a Hollywood Hills kind of home, a lot of vegetation around it, a pool down this walkway. There were a lot of animal skins. That is when all the amps were white. Jerry had this skin you put over your head, a caftan. I had the leopard outfit—it was part of our garb. There was a little guest house that Moose lived in—he was a friend of my brother's and mine from the early days who was working with the group as a tech. Sly had moved him down there to help him out. I remember those goofy gatherings, those Hollywood parties that you would see in a D movie at four in the morning. All the wrong people.

VERNON "MOOSE" CONSTAN: I was living with him when he was first living up on Coldwater Canyon. He liked having me around because he used to like to talk about his electronic ideas and how it could be made into his equipment. I modified it all. It was my idea to build a tall stage with a smooth front. Before that, you could always climb the front of the stage. He always liked to be right at the edge of the stage. There were white rugs. All the amplifiers were redone in white Naugahyde. He wore a lot of white leather.

STEPHANI OWENS: We had some intimate times, I will say that, but I was never his girlfriend. I was more his conscience. I never took on the attitude of being his woman because it would have made me less effective in the things that I was supposed to do. For myself, I needed to know that I was there to take care of the business and be a contribution to what the whole group was about. Once I put myself in the position of being his woman, then I lost some of that leverage. That was not something that I could comfortably do. I was in and out a lot because he wanted our relationship to be one where he could control me as a woman.

I wanted him to respect me for what I could contribute, and for my mind. I've always been very opinionated and have a difficult time dealing with anybody that wanted me to think their way as opposed to what I felt myself and what I knew to be right and wrong. I always wanted to be in a position with Sly where I could tell him that he was wrong without having to suffer any serious repercussions. There were a lot of times where I played that role. And I was the woman on his arm, being cute and not really functioning in a business sense that was visible.

KITSAUN KING: Sly came over to our house to meet our parents. If you want to do it right, if this is something that you are serious about, then you go and meet the parents. This is how he was raised. He was courtly. He came over with his little dog, Shadow. Sly was totally into dogs. He ended up with I don't know how many dogs, ten or something. Deb was young, going off all the way across the country with some musician. It caused concern, as it would for any parents. Something you think about, something you take note of. When we moved to L.A., that is when my father got really nervous. I was going to Europe to meet my high school girlfriend. I was going to meet her and we were going to travel all over Europe together. I had the ticket, the whole thing. I was going to stop in L.A., visit my sister, and then take off. I stopped in L.A. and never left. Ended up returning my ticket, collecting the money.

JERRY MARTINI: When Sly moved to L.A., that is when it all started happening because of all the bad influences of all the dealers around him. The entourage really got in the way. Through all this he still had a lot of creativeness left in him. He still had a lot of brains. He was still a brilliant man. He was still writing some good songs then. It was just that he was so distracted by negative people. He was such a nice guy, such a caring guy, and so far ahead of his time. Once you get around the drug people, they will bring you down into the hole that they are not trying to climb out of.

HAMP "BUBBA" BANKS: When I got out of jail, Sly got in touch with me and said, "Bub, I need you, man." I had a Lincoln and a house I gave away. J.B.—my friend James Vernon Brown—and I went together. He was in Coldwater Canyon at Isaac Hayes's house. The first night I was there, he introduced me and I got my propers. There was a girl there who I think was supposed to be Freddie's girl or something—Stephani's best friend, Lenora. Stephani was Sly's woman, so, quite naturally, her friend was Freddie's girl because he was next in command. When I came in, I told her to pick something off the floor. She said something. I said something back. She said, "I'm going to pick that up and then I am going." I said, "As long as you do it in that order, great." She picked whatever it was off the floor and left. I became, at that point, somebody down there that everybody had to reckon with.

JAMES VERNON "J.B." BROWN: We flew in, limousine picked us up, took us up to Coldwater Canyon. I hadn't seen him in years. He had become Sly and the Family Stone. We got there and it was a twenty-four-hour party. For days. It was just such an amazing thing to be sitting up in this huge house on Mulholland Drive. At that point, that's when the decision was made that Bubba and I would come on board. He wanted us to run his concerts and be with him. We sort of picked up the ball and ran with it, which scared the hell out of Dave Kapralik because we were street guys. But Dave couldn't do anything about it. So there we were touring around the country with Sly and literally sitting in on the deals with William Morris and Columbia Records and really managing what was taking place.

HAMP "BUBBA" BANKS: It had skyrocketed above my comprehension. They were in a million-dollar house and I moved right in. Sly made everybody understand that I was the one. Nothing happened without me. I did interviews, called people in, put anybody out. I didn't care. When it got too big for me, I knew the cat that knew the cat that could get it done. That made me the cat, period.

When I got to Los Angeles, he was the cocaine king. I saw him going down Hollywood Boulevard with a little violin case and he looked like the Morton salt woman. Cocaine was just falling out the back of it. The cat had gotten so big, as big as life. He was doing what he wanted. He had places over there and he used to make jokes about going from Coldwater to Commonwealth, because we were on Coldwater and Stephani and them was on Commonwealth. He trusted me. Now he could really do what he wanted. He could pass out. Before he would pass out, he would say, "Where's Bub?" That was all he wanted to know—where's Bub?—and if I was in the house, he could do what he wanted. He didn't have to lock no doors. I was there.

JAMES VERNON "J.B." BROWN: It was full of guns before we got there. Sly wanted to be one of them dudes, that was his problem. Sly was playing at being a gangster. They would like to believe that we had that influence on him. When we arrived, they wanted a fall guy. They wanted me and Bubba to be the fall guys, but we had nothing to do with it. Left up to us, he wouldn't have done any of those things.

Sly, Winterland, 1971.

DAVID KAPRALIK: I had horse blinders on. Sly's personal life, the ladies, I couldn't have cared less. I had no interest. I never focused in on the ladies around him or the bodyguards. Sly always protected me from a lot of that. Sly was very controlling. When submachine guns were in plain view, that wasn't reassuring that I was in the Land of Oz. Coldwater Canyon is when it became very evident. I kept a place in New York, but I opened an office in L.A. That was Stone Flower Productions just across from the Capitol Records tower. Stephani was with us. Barbara was with us. Steve Topley was a promotion man who worked for Epic, then I hired him away. A lot of heavy shit went down. It was also when we started other productions. Sly produced Little Sister. We managed the group 61X, nice kids. Joe Hicks was an R&B singer friend of Sly's. Sly produced the record under our Scepter deal. Florence Greenberg, God bless her soul, she gave us a hefty advance and Sly produced Joe Hicks, who didn't happen. I had no control over what Sly was doing at that point. I affected it, but Sly did the production.

"HAMP BUBBA" BANKS: His sister Loretta was there in the beginning [1969], running things for Sly. She was there because she was smart. He was trying to build things that he could trust. But when anything gets big, your trust mechanism says, "Someone is trying to get me." Loretta said that Sly is the devil and they had that kind of thing. I think he got scared of her, she had this psychic-type thing. She started making these little moves that Sly was scared of. He got rid of her, fired her. They didn't get along. Loretta never did fit—she was the devil. She was over at Stone Flower. Joe Hicks was over there. Everybody loved Hicks sincerely, but Sly took Joe Hicks's woman, too. Then they became, well, not exactly enemies. Joe Hicks still used to come around. Like most of the dudes that came around Sly, he always had a little satchel.

He had Marvin Braxton, the other group [6IX]. Little Sister had a hit record. When they looked like they were getting too big, no more. He didn't do any follow-up on anything he did. Little Sister didn't go no further. Two songs—"Somebody's Watching You" and "You're the One"—then Little Sister became the backup group to Sly and the Family Stone.

STEPHEN PALEY: He had a production deal at Atlantic called Stone Flower, and he produced Little Sister and Joe Hicks and a group called 6IX. He started making different kinds of records for them. It was all electronic music. He started with a rhythm machine, instead of using Gregg on drums, and I think that he played bass himself on those records because he played bass in a very distinctive way, which was better for those records than Larry Graham's bass. That concept carried over to the *Riot* album, which was an extension of that.

VAETTA STEWART: We had Sly's songs and our own. "You're the One," "Somebody's Watching You," "Hot Fun in the Summertime," and some very old songs, and some of the things we just made up as we went along. Some of the things, we brought from church because we all attended the same type of church. We didn't last out on our own a long time. I think we basically stopped for lack of management. I functioned on my family's schedule. When they stopped, I stopped. I can't give you any specific reason, other than when they stopped, so did I.

ELVA "TINY" MOUTON: Vet and I recorded with Sly on the very first recording, *A Whole New Thing*. "Everyday People," "Hot Fun in the Summertime," you name it, all of the hits and some of the things that never made it to wax. "Somebody's Watching You" was recorded on one of his albums, and we rerecorded that. But "You're the One" was kind of our own, and that was great fun. We were these young girls with this inexhaustible amount of energy. When we weren't singing background we were in the corner boogying down. We were part of Sly and the Family Stone. We performed on the shows as a part of the group. We did that for a long time. When Vet and I graduated from high school in 1969, we had the option. If Sly thought this was not a major concert or I don't need all these voices, we could stay home. We were also, during that time, newlyweds and having our first children. We were wanting to stay home with the kids. Family was starting to pull us.

DAVID KAPRALIK: Jerry is the one who told me that in Boston some [Black] Panther members tried to get Syl to drop me, get rid of whitey, get rid of the devil. He wouldn't hear of it. Even though I would say that our dialogue changed on one level, he would never entertain the idea of dropping me. The Panthers were after him. Sister Loretta, at this point, came into the picture. She was one of those voices trying to split him from me. Even though he was being truculent with me, abrasive at times, he was still wearing that star of David I gave him. There were forces trying to break us up. She didn't trust me. She didn't know me. She was the eldest child and the only nonperforming member of the family. This was her opportunity to have a degree of power. Of course, there was a lot of drugs going on in this period. It was just about that time I was introduced to cocaine. Cocaine is a well-known antidote to pain, and I started to do a lot of drugs.

JERRY MARTINI: That is when Redd Foxx had his club on La Cienega. He had a little garage in the back where he had his office, just like on *Sanford and Son*. He would tell jokes. We all had these little vials. Sly poured out a gram vial to give Redd some. 'Thank you, man," he said. "You got any for y'all?" and he sniffed up the whole thing. He did a gram in one sniff. "Whoa, hose nose," said Sly.

STEPHANI OWENS: There was a guy in L.A., he was like a psychologist who lived up in the hills, and we could go there and buy bottles of pills in quantities of five hundred a shot. Sly had a safe in his upstairs bedroom at Coldwater that had these bottles of five hundred pills in them. All downers. The only upper that they ever dealt with was the cocaine. The worst part was when it came time for them to get on stage with all these pills that were being passed around and the droopiness—okay, it is time to get on stage now—and trying to get their energy up. Sly could be falling down on the floor in the dressing room—I would be trying to pick him up to get him on stage—but once he got on stage, the crowd got him going. There were a couple of incidents that I could see the pills were taking effect, but for the most part, if he got on stage and the crowd did its thing, he would come alive. He would get into it with the group, get off stage, and then he would be back down to the downers.

HAMP "BUBBA" BANKS: Stephani was making hats. That was during the hat-making days where everybody wore hats. Stephani made the hats. If you had a girlfriend, that was her job, making hats. Going to the gig, coming from the gig, make a hat.

JAMES VERNON "J.B." BROWN: I called myself a concert coordinator because I wanted to be more than his bodyguard. He would take you into situations that would blow you away. You'd go there and people would have guns or whatever. There was an instance where we went with Richard Pryor to this house and this guy pulled a gun on me and stuck it up to my head. I told him, "You are a punk because you would have shot me, so obviously, you are not a killer." Sly had to grab me and take me out of the house, but I felt that if I hadn't have been who I am, he might have shot me.

HAMP "BUBBA" BANKS: Sly sat down with me and said that I had to get Rose back. He and Freddie never did like Larry being with Rose. That's who Rose stayed with in New York. They shared a bedroom. They both had their own houses, so she would stay with him and vice versa. Larry was trying to be a Sly in his own right. It wasn't my plan. They couldn't control her. I was the only person who they knew could control her. I called Rose while they were there. The last time I saw her, I was angry. "I'm not going to tell you that I have changed," I told her, "that I'm another dude. I'm the same person. I'm coming to Oakland. Pick me up at the airport."

Sly and them got me to the airport and Rose picked me up. The first thing she asked me, "What did you bring?"—meaning drugs. I hadn't, but I did put something together. I really wasn't into it. I never tried to fatten no frog for no snake. When I got there that night, I put something together and she snorted cocaine. I think that was Larry's little thing on her because she wasn't a person who could get drugs. As long as she was band oriented, she could get her little toots. I got her back. The first night I slept on top of the covers. At least I made it to the bed. I think this went on for three days. She was still doing her superstar thing. The first part of our relationship, I would always jam her about Larry because I really wanted a confrontation. I knew I never would get one because he was a card-carrying coward, so I didn't sweat it. Like I said, she was more man than he would ever be.

SEVEN

THE RIOT WAS
ALREADY GOING ON

Sly, Oakland Airport, 1971.

AL DEMARINO: Regrettably, we had a cancellation at the Trenton Armory and it was promoted by a Black promoter, a street fellow by the name of Dickie Diamond, who had been doing dates at the Armory successfully. He wasn't a Johnny-come-lately. He wasn't a new promoter on the block. He was working the Trenton marketplace well. He was a street guy with a lot of connections. He felt that he was given very late notification. We had suggested making up the date, rescheduling it in the immediate future. We had a hard time with the rest of the schedule at the time, the other regions of the country that the band was going to play, figuring out how we were going to get an East Coast date in a New Jersey marketplace to fit in naturally routing-wise with the schedule. He got impatient waiting and he waited and he waited. As the wait continued, he got threatening.

To make a long story short, finally, from street sources, he found out that Sly was coming in. He wanted to confront Sly, not necessarily threaten him, but he wanted reimbursement immediately, rather than wait for a new rescheduled date. He was, in effect, reaching a point of threatening. So I scheduled a meeting for him in my office. We had no intention of having Sly present—we didn't know how heated it might get and we would never put an artist in that situation. Sly felt since he knew that it was becoming a street situation, if you will, that he would send some of his buddies over who were traveling with the band who could relate to this.

HAMP "BUBBA" BANKS: First time I went to New York, I was scared to death. I'm a local boy and when I got to the big city like that, I was scared. Me and J.B., we go to Al DeMarino's office and there was a dude in there, Dickie Diamond, who was obviously a promoter. He had promoted a gig and Sly didn't show.

JAMES VERNON "J.B." BROWN: So Dickie Diamond walks in the room with this seven-foot gargantuan giant with him. He comes in and starts talking to us, and I say, "Wait a minute, I don't know who the fuck you think you are, but if you mad at Sly, you need to go over to the Hilton and be mad at Sly—I'm not the guy." The guy says, "We are going to blow you away.'" I says, "I am going to grab your big ass and we are going to fall out of these thirty-two floors."

HAMP "BUBBA" BANKS: The guy said, "Man, cut the shit, this motherfucker owes me for a gig. I did a gig, and I paid this motherfucker, and he didn't show. I am out on murder one for appeal, and I'm trying to get my thing together." We got into a thing in his office. That is when it becomes killing talk. We are up on the thirty-second floor. He's mad. I got to get mad. He's probably got a gun. I don't know what the situation is.

AL DEMARINO: So Hamp and J.B. met with me and Dickie in my office and it did indeed become heated. Dickie Diamond had, I don't want to call him a bodyguard, but somebody who did work with him for protective purposes. There were some very, very tense moments. Voices were raised and it got heated at one point. J.B. jumped up and I literally thought that I was going to see a body flying from the thirty-second floor through my plate-glass window.

HAMP "BUBBA" BANKS: I hooked up a date with him to redo the date that he lost. We went back to the hotel. J.B. and I felt like heroes and we are trying to get to Sly to tell him what he got us into. We wound up having to kick the door down. I woke him and Stephani up.

JAMES VERNON "J.B." BROWN: Now I am mad because Sly's got me in front of these gangsters. I go over to the hotel and Sly is locked up in the room. I get the manager to bring a lock thing up and we had to cut the chain on his door. I said, "What's the deal? Why didn't you go over to William Morris?" He's laughing. I said "I'm outta here" and I jumped on a plane and went back to California. I said this boy is a fool and that is what he was.

HAMP "BUBBA" BANKS: We wait until he's got his little hit [snorts]. Everybody knows you can't fuck with him until he has his little hit. Then he says, "Dickie Diamond pooted y'all." When he said that, I just wanted to say, "You gotta be kidding, man." Sly was so arrogant. We left him in New York.

KITSAUN KING: Just prior to him moving to L.A., as it turned out, the person that I was dating at that time, Jay, had some friends who wanted to turn us on to this new drug, PCP. At that time, they were calling it angel dust. We tried it and it was the most horrible high I ever had in my life. Shortly after that, I think it was Jay, my boyfriend, who turned Sly on to this. That was the beginning of the end. Shortly after that, Sly moved to L.A. When he got to L.A., I think that whole angel dust thing was bigger down there than it was up here.

FREDDIE STEWART: Coldwater Canyon, every night that I was there, something was going on. A lot of people all the time. Always a party, day and night. Lot of drugs. When you say PCP, I remember New Year's Eve 1969. Debbie's friend Jay and little Jerry almost died by taking it. I remember Sly coming downstairs saying, "Look, we are partying. I have cocaine, this is what I have.

This other guy here has something else. I am not trying that. I am not messing with it. If you want to mess with it, you are on your own. This is what I have." He made it very clear. Everybody heard. The house was packed, everywhere, every room. Upstairs, his room, around the side in the back room where I was staying, or in the living room, on the patio, all around the other side, the other two rooms in the back. People everywhere. But he made it clear. I have cocaine and this guy has something else. Of all the people that tried it, they had to rush two people to the hospital.

HAMP "BUBBA" BANKS: It all fell apart at Coldwater. That is when Sly did the PCP and he was just out of it. He was all the way out. There wasn't anything happening no more. It was over. He was through. He was doing shit you would expect to see in some kind of institution for mentally retarded people. He and Freddie walked around the house all day like zombies. I started sleeping with a pistol. I was going to shoot Freddie one night. I was sitting in the living room playing backgammon and Sly was full of PCP. He stood behind me and said, "Bub" and I knew that shit had got him. I said, "What?" He said, "Phone book." I kept playing. He said it again, "Phone book." I looked at him, and he was rigid. I said, "Oh, you want your phone book." Now why I would have his phone book, I have no idea. I ran upstairs and when I came downstairs, I had a pistol. I said, "Motherfuck you, your phone book, the horse you rode in on." He said, "Bub, put the gun down." I don't have a problem with that. Freddie said, "Let me hold the gun." "You're the one I got the gun for," I said, "because I ain't worried about this fool." Sly ran up the stairs and locked himself in his room and didn't come out for three or four days. They were gone then. Anyway, that is where it all fell apart.

JAMES VERNON "J.B." BROWN: From the PCP to the shit he was taking, he went nuts. The family, to me, was one of the most hypocritical things that I had ever seen. I thought it was a sad situation because you respected them, thinking they are church and their religious thing was valid. But you watched them allow all this crap to take place—Sly fucking Cynthia, just the weirdest stuff you ever want to see. But KC never said nothing.

STEPHANI OWENS: He had gotten into PCP, angel dust. There was a young White girl who came from a very rich family and was into equestrian riding. She had it all. She was eighteen and driving a Mercedes. She was following Sly around. He turned her on to PCP. She got so strung out on it. We hadn't seen her in a while and I called her mother's house, just to find out how she was doing. She didn't really want to talk to me, other than to say that her daughter had always spoke very highly of me. Her mother said that she had been in the hospital, that she had a total breakdown, and was learning to write her name again. Total breakdown from this drug.

I remember hanging up the phone, being in tears, going and finding Sly's stash, and flushing it down the toilet. He, of course, went berserk, but I didn't give a shit. It's bad shit.

At that point, I felt like I was on the edge. I knew that this drug was ugly because of what it did. I experimented with it. It took you to another place. You weren't walking on the ground anymore. I told him that you can't do this and still make music. It is going to kill you. I took it and flushed it down. I didn't admit to it at first. I just did it on the sneak side, but I ended up telling him, like I always did. He was frantically looking for it and I said I just got rid of it. I told him I flushed it down the toilet. He wasn't happy about it, but I thought that he would get much more angry than he did. I thought he was going to totally go off, but he didn't really do that.

There were no real repercussions for me doing that, blowing whatever money it cost. People gave him stuff. Drugs were just there. He didn't even have to ask for it. He didn't have to buy. There were some drugs that were bought, but not as much as were given to him. It really had a big influence on everything that was going on. There was no real separation between life and drugs. Life was drugs, and it was music. They would spend so many hours— thirty-six to forty-eight hours—in a stretch at the Record Plant, wearing out the engineers. But they were doing drugs, too.

HAMP "BUBBA" BANKS: I was trying to commit Freddie and he hit me in my head. I was taking him to the nuthouse. I was taking Sly. It wasn't about Freddie. But Sly got to the top of the stairs when it was time to go and that was it. Freddie was there. Since I had made the arrangements, I took him, put him in the car, and his daddy went with me. We were riding on the freeway, he looked over at me and, wham, he hit me. I pulled over and I was going to beat his ass. I pulled over and thought about it. I'm going to pull over to get in a fight with him and I am taking him to the nuthouse? Who should be going, me or him?

When we get to the place, he straightened up. He wasn't fucked up no more. We got in there and he started seeing real nuts. I was talking to the people about him staying at the facility. His daddy was there, but he just probably needed the ride because he didn't have anything to do with it. I asked them to see the facility. That scared him to death. Freddie said, "I don't want to stay here." Once it got to the PCP part, it was over. That got pitiful. It wasn't about music. We were through. Sly had become a vegetable and so had Freddie. KC was still around there looking for somebody to blame shit on, rather than take the reins. He was looking for me, J.B., anybody but Sly. Sly was always the victim, he never was the one. He only messed with drugs because somebody gave it to him. Well, that was his reason for eating dinner, too. He never was responsible for nothing, except being the hero.

KITSAUN KING: Gun the pit bull was, unfortunately, just as schizophrenic as the adults in the house that he moved into. Gun was just too far inbred. Gun was a stone nut. We saw Gun attack other dogs and that was bad enough. You would have to get the hose and brooms. He would attack anything that had a hat on. Men would come in with hats and Gun was on them. I don't know what he didn't like about hats, but he had something up his butt about hats. He was pretty mellow with women. Maybe it was the male energy. I'm not sure what would set him off, but the hat thing definitely would. He was fine, then somebody would come in like Joe Hicks or somebody with a hat on, and he lost his mind. He didn't get to the point of attacking Joe, but he got all flipped out.

Gun started chasing his tail. He wouldn't stop. Literally, all day chasing his tail. At that time, a bee's nest had been discovered in the eaves in the ceiling in the living room at Coldwater. The bee people came and got the beehive out. That was a big drama right there. We thought that Gun had somehow gotten stung on his tail. Took him to the vet and checked that out. There were no stings. I don't know if the vet came up with this or Sly had the idea of cutting his tail off. They do sometimes show this dog without a tail in the show world. The vet had tried a lot of things. The dog would not stop chasing his tail. They cut the tail off. He came home, he just chased his butt.

JAMES VERNON "J.B." BROWN: We went to one house one night and this was the head of the Mafia at Long Island. When we landed at La Guardia at Butler Aviation, there's nothing but limousines waiting for us, all these big Italian guys and me and Sly. They escort us to Long Island, to this guy's house. It was so dark that you could barely see in front of your hand. If you ever go to those Italian joints in New York where the mob hangs out, you know that you can't see until you get up on somebody. We went through this tunnel and up to this guy's bedroom, who was the big guy. Sly jumps on the bed with this guy and his wife. This guy has got to be in his fifties or sixties. They are negotiating. The next thing, J.R. came into the picture. J.R. was truly a gangster. J.R. and his brothers, they were gangsters.

JERRY MARTINI: J.R. was the bodyguard. He took me on his route with him. He used to collect. He took me in his Caddy to all of the stripper joints all over New York. He would have a drink and collect the money. I'd look up at the dancers and he would say, "You want one?" He respected the band members. He was there to protect the band. He worked for Sly mainly, but once I was sitting at Sly's house, in what used to be my room before he took it away and gave it to Bubba. I was sitting on the floor talking about something and a guy came up behind me, grabbed me by the hair and neck, and dragged me out of the room, saying, "Get the fuck out of my friend's room." J.R. walked into the room and said, "He's in the band—don't fuck with the band."

HAMP "BUBBA" BANKS: J.R. Vatrano became more of the bodyguard once he got he got into it, and I became more of a personal manager. Sly flew up to San Francisco one night to buy drugs with J.R. and myself. J.R. did whatever Sly did. J.R. stayed with him. Sly got pickled and we got the red-eye flight back to Los Angeles. We are in first class and Sly has a tape—he always had a tape. The stewardess came up and said that he was going to have to turn that down a little bit because people on the plane was asleep. Sly didn't even acknowledge her. She walked off. He turned it up louder and she went and got the pilot. He came back and told Sly that he was going to have to turn down the music. He said something smart and the pilot walked off after Sly turned it down. When he walked off, Sly blasted it. The pilot turned around and they scuffled a little bit on the plane. J.R. grabbed the pilot. That was his job. I knew that when this plane landed, there were going to be so many police officers. Sly started talking to some girl on the plane and was smart enough to give her his drugs. When we got off the plane, they didn't know who to stop. We made it out to the streets.

DAVID KAPRALIK: After the first appearance at Madison Square Garden, the night after the triumphant appearance which produced reviews that were stunning in their impact replete with references to the fascistic energies that were evoked with this towering charismatic figure, the next night I had booked him into a Black theater in Newark, New Jersey. It seemed to me, in retrospect, that this was such a comedown for him. This was the first time that I recall him raging at me for booking him there. This was followed, a short time after, by their appearance at Constitution Hall with Daughters of the American Revolution and there was some kind of fracas that took place there. Another cause that evoked his rage. He started manifesting rage for being booked where he was. From that point on, the nature of our relationship changed.

GREGG ERRICO: The not showing up stuff kind of snuck up, slipped in. It started out with us being late a couple of times. We were drawing real good. The group was making significant noise.

But Sly would always take an experience and, if he could do something with the experience or get something out of it, manipulate it in a different way, he would. We were late and it would create a tension. The promoter would be nervous. The audience would be nervous. Everybody was trying to get the band there. There was a tension. He kind of took that. Actually, that tension that was created by being late and nobody knew what was going to happen; it created a thing that once you were there and did your thing, you got off a little more. After all was said and done and we played, it was cool. It was kind of like your relationship, if you fight with your old lady and then go make love. Real intense fight, really intense fuck, too. Same kind of thing. That was the beginning of it.

STEPHANI OWENS: He was never on time. It was always an effort to get them to the gig and get them on stage on time. It was a whole series of things. We would have to get on a plane, but there was lots of hoops we had to jump through to get them there. Rose you could always count on to be where she needed to be. It was mostly Freddie and Sly, because even when the rest of the group would catch the commercial flight and do what they were supposed to do, I would be trying to find a private plane for Freddie and Sly to go on. I would exhaust all majors for getting them on any mode of transportation to get them to the gig on time. Sometimes I would have to hire a private plane, helicopter, limousine. A lot of times the group would be there waiting when they showed up. Sly had a thing about wanting to have his brother with him. Or Freddie would say, "Is Sly ready to go? Because I'm not going unless Sly is there." Sometimes I would have to tell the group, go and I will deal with these two. It was easier to deal with two than eight. Sometimes KC would go if he knew that we were taking a commercial flight, because he was not into the small plane thing. There was a certain amount of trust that he would place on me that, even if he left his two sons behind, I would get them there eventually. As the escalation of drugs happened, so did the lateness of the gigs and cancellations.

HAMP "BUBBA" BANKS: Bobby Womack had a gig to do, and he said, "I have to go, man, I have a gig." Sly said, "Make 'em wait, Bobby. It is not the time, it is the timing." He philosophized this to everybody all the time. I told Bobby, "Get your ass outta here. I know you don't know how to leave, you do not know how to stand up—get the fuck outta here and go do your job." This was at a critical point in his career. He looked at me and thought about it. Like Sly, he always wanted to be the tough guy.

BOBBY WOMACK: We were riding, going somewhere. I had a date or an appointment, it was something important, and Sly said, "Why do you gotta make this?" I said that I got to follow through with my word, my word is my bond. He kept trying to tell me why I should make people wait—it would be more important, I would be more important. Bubba stepped in and said to me, "Do not listen to this man, don't even discuss it with him." That went a long way with me because Sly and Bubba were really tight. Bubba was speaking out totally against what [Sly] was trying to say.

VERNON "MOOSE" CONSTAN: He would say to me, "If I worked down at a drugstore and didn't feel like showing up that day, I probably wouldn't even get fired. Here I am a powerful person and I don't have the right to say I don't want to come." That was his reasoning for not going to a concert. Another one of his clichés was "Being sorry is for sorry people," so you would never get that word out of him.

JERRY MARTINI: It was pretty nightmarish. Granted a lot of gigs were canceled then. But what you don't know is that the band went. We were there. We showed up to a lot of gigs in 1970 that we didn't play. Once Freddie hooked up with him and they were hanging together, then it was hard to get them out of the house. One of Sly's girlfriends was quoted as saying that she had been in some of the nicest bathrooms in the world. That's where everybody hung, in the bathrooms. Very private. Solve all the world's problems in there. How could I be so stupid?

LARRY GRAHAM: There was a gig in Oakland where he didn't show up. I mean I was affected by stuff like that. This is home, so if there's a no-show, I got family and friends and stuff that I've got to deal with. I know that this no-show-late-thing got started, but why, I don't know. I don't know if the rest of the band knows. At Oakland, we were all down at the Holiday Inn at Hegenberger Road. Mountain was the group that went on, and I think they even played an extended set. We were all at the hotel. Unless someone in the band talked to him and knew what was going on, we were all in the same boat. To this day, I still don't know what went on, why he didn't show up. Mainly because I didn't ask.

GREGG ERRICO: The one that comes to mind was the show in Oakland. It was total chaos. We were at the Holiday Inn there. He had showed up in a helicopter. He was late. We were supposed to go on. We are at the hotel, getting ready to go to the Coliseum. By this time, we already knew what we were going to have to deal with—every time we would have to go to a gig, he was going to be late. Was he even in the same city yet? No, he was in L.A. But he was on his way in a jet. Then they were going to take him from the airport, which is a half-mile away, and land him in the parking lot of the Holiday Inn. It got to where there was this tension that was creating this excitement. It was like, if you were late, you got a police escort with the lights on and everything. Over the top. By this time, it was way past anything that made any sense. But he was able to keep on doing it and get away with it.

He finally arrived in a helicopter. By this time, we were into a good hour and a half, two hours, maybe more past start time. There were problems back at the Coliseum. He was too frazzled to go on. I just remember being disappointed; this is home, family, friends. This wasn't the first time because every time we came and played, after the group had some significant success, we would come back to San Francisco and give bad shows. Not good shows. Sly would be nervous to come back and play San Francisco.

DAVID KAPRALIK: I had them booked somewhere in the West, then Randall's Island, Queens, New York, and, two days later, I had them booked at Minneapolis. I needed, in order to fly them to Randall's Island, to charter a plane. The group had very little money. We weren't seeing any royalties because of unrecouped recording costs. I was pretty strapped, having put everything I had into the group. The promoters went south with the money. Randall's Island itself was contested turf, contested by a number of militant ethnic organizations. There was the Young Lords, the Puerto Rican militants; if not the Panthers, then another militant Black organization; it was also contested by an Italian ethnic group. The most vocal was the Young Lords. I could not afford to charter a plane to bring them to New York to do Randall's Island when there was no money. I held a press conference to announce that Sly was not going to be at the concert because I could not afford to bring them in. It was not Sly's fault this time. This was my decision. I was stuck on principle that I was going to make that statement.

I went there with all the bravado that I was capable of, with all the attitude adjuster I was ingesting at the time. The minute we went through the gate, I could see an ocean of bodies suddenly pressing the limousine. Before we knew it, they were rocking the limo. It was a scary moment, but I was determined to get on stage and make the announcement. I did, but not before I got out of the limousine and I was surrounded by microphones in my face. I had nothing to hide, no hidden agenda, and I had a story to tell. Suddenly I feel something very sharp in my ribs. I managed to get through that and get on stage to say my statement to a lot of catcalls and objects thrown in my direction.

> From *New York Times*, July 28, 1970, Chicago: "Several thousand youths battled the police for more than five hours yesterday evening, hurling rocks and roaming the Loop district smashing windows. The riot began shortly after 4:00 p.m. at a free rock concert in downtown Grant Park when the featured band, Sly and the Family Stone, refused to play. By 9:50 p.m. the police reported more than 150 arrests. At least twenty-five persons, including ten policemen, were treated at hospitals for injuries. Three young men were wounded by gunfire."

STEPHANI OWENS: The reason given for why the Chicago riot happened was that Sly was late, but that was not true. The truth was that we came into town and the riot started. We came in by limo and we came over a bridge. We were in contact with what was going on. We didn't do that gig because by the time we got there the riot had fully escalated. Our equipment men were already in there, had set up, and the show had been delayed. It was a free concert and there were other groups in front of Sly and the Family Stone. The other thing about the situation was the politics of having a free concert, which was not a popular thing. All of the police forces were there. The police lined up all along the stage. The story I heard from one of the equipment men was that somebody threw something behind the stage where they had all of these policemen, and the police threw it back at them. Then they made all these bogus announcements about Sly being late.

VERNON "MOOSE" CONSTAN: The police started charging. They made their way up to the bandstand and started tear-gassing the place. We were in the rooms in the back, the tear gas all around us, laying on the floor. But a lot of people were in big misery because they were standing and started crying and rubbing their eyes. We got out of there, I did. We looked outside and they had a police car turned over, burning. There were three things burning. This was two hours before Sly was supposed to come on. So I called him up and said, "I don't know—they are tipping over cars."

STEPHANI OWENS: We were in the city on time and were stopped by the police when we came across the bridge. They said you cannot go in there—we are going to hold you here until we figure out what the situation is. We sat there for a long time. He first wanted all of us to go in because he thought that they could still do the concert. But when it got to the point where they said that we could not do the concert, he said that he wanted to go in anyway and make sure that his people got out all right. He thought that he could stop whatever it was that was going on. They would not allow that. They said if he wanted to go in, they'd have to put him in a paddy wagon. At that point, they were already beating up the police and knocking over police cars. Sly ended up going in a paddy wagon. They made the rest of us stay in the cars. None of that was ever talked about.

JERRY MARTINI: We got blamed for the riot in Grant Park in Chicago. It was not our fault. We were told to be there at a certain time and we drove all night to get there on time. We got there what I would consider early and the riot was already going on. We offered to rent a helicopter to fly in and play, but they wouldn't let us. Mayor Daley didn't want any more concerts then. We were used as a scapegoat because of our reputation. It was simple—who better to blame? You tell the band to come at a certain time and then advertise another time. Somebody should have been aware of that on our team. It was a mess up on our team. We were there and we were totally ready to play, Sly was ready. We got blamed for that on page one. The paper printed a retraction on page forty-three or something. That just ruined us, ruined our careers.

GREGG ERRICO: There was one in the Midwest, nighttime, whiter, the audience had already been there for two hours. They were yelling, screaming, stamping their feet. We got word. There was some tension between Larry and Freddie. We pulled off the road. They actually spilled out of the car and into the street and got into a fight. Swings. We even had our garb on and Freddie's got ripped. Got it out of the way. We looked at each other, shook hands, ran up to the stage, and did a great show. This had been building for a while, maybe months.

JERRY MARTINI: When Rose got mad and didn't go on one Europe tour, Vet said that she had a blonde wig. She put it on and everybody thought she was Rose. When Vet opens up to you, she is a lot of fun. Her voice was too low to be a great singer. She took Rose's part, but nobody could take Rose's place. She sang on all of Rose's parts, not the real high parts, but she covered. She had the visual thing.

HAMP "BUBBA" BANKS: They sent Vet. I might have got into an argument with Sly or somebody, whatever, about Rose, and I didn't let her go. I took her out of the group. So he took Vet. And when they came back, we did our makeup, whatever the reason was. When they came back, it started all over again. She didn't have to be in it anymore once I made that move. I became her personal manager, as far as the group went. I was really Sly's personal manager, because you didn't talk to Sly—you talked to me. He didn't talk to nobody.

DAVID KAPRALIK: I think Cobo Hall in Detroit was the one for me. On the verge of riot and I knew that Sly was in his motel room and I knew what he was doing. I'm backstage, the promoter, head of security, the hall manager, one of them making his point by poking his finger in my breast plate. "Get that guy here." It hurt. I was helpless, and at that point, I realized it was hopeless to get him from the motel to the concert. I gave up. I knew that if I didn't give up, I would be dead.

EIGHT

GUNS AND DOGS

Sly, Santa Clara County Fairgrounds, 1971.

STEPHANI OWENS: We moved to Bel Air [by fall 1971]. It used to be the house of John and Michelle Phillips. When we first moved into that house, there were rooms that had some things in them that made us think the house was haunted. We found a Ouija board in there. We found different pieces of paperwork that made us believe they were into witchcraft. When Sly moved into that house, a lot of band members moved in there with him because it was the first house he had that was really huge. They were in the course of recording at that time. Jerry, the sax player, and his lady, Lynne, lived in this room that was kind of like a sitting room with a bedroom off to the side. Freddie stayed there for a while. Hamp da Bubba da Banks and J.B. were there because this house had tons of room in it. We fixed up a room for KC back behind the kitchen that had been the maid's quarters. The kitchen was humongous. They had a wine cellar. Part of my job was to explore all the rooms in the house and get them furnished into a living situation. Going down into the cellar, they still had wine down there.

One day, when Sly had moved in but we were still getting the house together, it came time to fix a meal. I went to the store and got some chickens. I went down to the wine cellar and pulled out a bottle of wine to bake the chicken in. I seasoned it up and poured a little bit of the wine on the chicken and stuck it in the oven. There was this guy whose wife had died named Jim Ford. He was a White guy, kind of country, who played the guitar—a redneck kind of guy, really down home. But he knew about wines. He walked into the kitchen and saw this bottle of wine sitting on the counter. He looked at the bottle and asked, "Where is the rest of this wine?" I said, "It is in the chicken." He said, "You mean to tell me you took this bottle of wine and are baking the chicken with it? This is a very rare bottle of wine." I had no clue. It turned out to be the best chicken that anybody ever had. And he ended up drinking the rest of the bottle.

Bel Air had one room with a pool table where everybody spent a lot of time. On the ground floor, there was the kitchen, pool room, KC's room, living room, library, and another little room off to the side that had a fireplace in it. The next floor above had the master bedroom for Sly and this other strange room where he put a Jacuzzi. Then there was the third floor that was almost like an attic with a staircase that went up to another level, where the studio was. The grounds were gorgeous. There was a garage with the chauffeur's apartment.

STEPHEN PALEY: What I thought was funny is that there would be these tour buses that stopped in front of the house all the time. These old ladies would get out. I said, "Sly, isn't that interesting that old ladies like that would be interested in your house?" He said that Jeanette MacDonald used to live there and that is why they were stopping to see it. It was an English Tudor house, 783 Bel Air. It was a rather grand house, beautiful lawns. The neighbors weren't thrilled about having Sly there.

EDWARD ELLIOTT ("EDDIE CHIN"): Sandy Duncan lived next door and that gate hadn't been closed in years. When we came up there, she closed the gate for the first time. *The Beverly Hillbillies* used to film across the street.

JERRY MARTINI: It was a stately mansion in Bel Air. The day that we moved in, it looked like the Munsters' place because John and Michelle Phillips had just moved out and left everything. They left their children's birth certificates. That is how fucked up they were. I found an ounce of cocaine there. I found LSD, all kinds of drugs, letters. They left it an absolute mess. My second wife, who was Portuguese, worked a miracle to fix that place up and make it look gorgeous. It was beautifully furnished, an incredible place, kind of gothic-looking, dark. Back in those days we loved that. Jimmy Ford was down there, who I kind of liked. We were all crazy, but Jimmy Ford was kind of positive. He was just one of the characters that turned up in Sly's life. Sly liked unique people. Sly collected people and I was one of them. Before, we were friends. But later, I was part of his collection of guns, dogs, people, things, cars, animals. He had a baboon. Gun killed the baboon, then fucked it.

HAMP "BUBBA" BANKS: Sly was the controller. Nobody was allowed to have their own blow. He was the man and that is where he got his audience. I was his pit bull that lived good. Whatever he said, it got handled. I didn't care what it was. It was handled. It wasn't nobody else but me. The girls had to check with me. Stephani was there when I got there. But once I got there, from that point on, I had not one problem. I called the shots and nobody double-checked me. Nobody had to check with Sly if I said something.

JERRY MARTINI: He talked me into literally boarding up my house in Marin County when he moved to Bel Air and coming down. He tried to pull it together as friends again. "Come on down and let's do it again, let's make it like the old days." I went for it. I became a coke addict, drug addict, vegetable, sitting around waiting for my line like the rest of the assholes. At his house, with my second wife, turned both of us into idiots, zombies.

HAMP "BUBBA" BANKS: When Sly would go off with who he wanted and lock the door, it was "no more drugs, let's shut down for the night." Everybody started bumping into each other, milling around. The store was closed. You would hear Freddie at the door, "Hey, Syl, can I talk to you?"

FREDDIE STEWART: At the Bel Air house, in the studio upstairs in the loft, a lot of times I tried to play and I would be too gone to play. Other kinds of things were going on. At the pool house, we had about eighteen guns. Kept them in one place. We had briefcase rifles, all kinds of stuff. Three or four cottages on the property, something else going on in each cottage. All the time. But it was dark. Dark, dark time. I got in a fight with the guy from Redbone, a guy just working at the pool. My dad used to come down and cool things off. He was good for that. When he could come. At that point, no one wanted to do anything. That was a dark period.

DAVID KAPRALIK: Dark, gloomy. The first thing that comes to mind is Gun. Gun was his dog and I have quite a way with dogs. He used Gun to intimidate people. I was never intimidated by Gun. I played with Gun, which pissed Sly off enormously. I was not personally intimidated by Bubba or bodyguards. I knew that I had no reason to fear them. They made me uncomfortable because I don't like guns. But I loved Gun the dog. I was blown away on cocaine. Sly would sit, imperially and imperiously, with lines in front of him, white lines and a line of people with their nostrils extended out to the spoon that he was offering. I was right there in the line, I admit. One moment, I hear a lot of screaming, a lot of noise, and in the living room someone had brought in a big boxer. Gun and this dog were at it. I remember walking between them.

Maybe if I had not been in the state that I was in, I wouldn't have done it. All the pain I was in, all the pain around me. My vision had disintegrated by this point. Sly's productivity was suffering, to put it mildly. I had no influence over what Sly was doing. I never had control. I never tried to have control. I had influence over Sly. I was managing the unmanageable. I influenced.

KITSAUN KING: You expected people like the David Kapraliks and the Steve Topleys—the people who were adults, had been in the music business, and who, in theory, had some knowledge—to be telling Sly the truth. But they weren't telling Sly the truth. They were just going along with Sly's program. And Sly's program was totally substandard because he was high all the time. Not because he didn't have a good idea or a brain, but because he was high. You can't make proper decisions when you are high. Not the kind of high he was.

STEPHANI OWENS: When I first went to work for Sly, I thought that David was really in charge of things. He and Sly seemed to have a good relationship with Dave having a good background in the music industry and vast connections with people, and actually laying on a plan for the escalation for Sly and the Family Stone. As time went on, records sold more, the crowds got larger, and the fees got larger, David ended up being a subservient person. Sly could talk him into anything. Ultimately, David got to the point where he felt that he could no longer handle Sly.

KITSAUN KING: At a point when I couldn't find a promoter in the country to touch Sly, my attorney, Peter Bennett, put me together with Ken Roberts. Peter, who I trusted and listened to relatively unquestioned, told me to meet with this guy and I did. He took a chance in promoting Sly. He is not someone whom I would have an easy rapport with. We were from different worlds. I assumed he was a concert promoter. I never questioned his background, his affiliations, his associations. He was purely filling a functional need I had. I don't want to use the word desperate. I was feeling enormous pressure from Sly and the group to get them booked. I turned to Ken. He booked them. He and Sly spoke the same kind of street language. I called him "the saint who came along." It was euphemistic and far from accurate, but he came along. I didn't know who else to turn to.

KEN ROBERTS: I took on two concerts with Sly and the Family Stone because nobody would promote him anymore, no one would buy him, no one would take him. I liked Sly as a performer. I knew his reputation, but that was my forte—taking on things that other people thought were too much trouble. That goes all the way back to when everybody thought Frankie Valli was through. I was his concert promoter, then his manager. Same thing with Sly. A lot of people thought that he was a big risk and he was never going to show up. I put him in Philadelphia in the Spectrum on Sunday. Then Saturday night we did West Virginia. That was the first weekend of January 1971. I felt a little secure with it because Al was a good friend of mine and I was familiar with a lot of the things that went on because of Kapralik and Peter Bennett, a lawyer who represented Kapralik at that time. He also represented me because I introduced him to Frankie Valli and the Four Seasons. I knew that they were fighting and having problems.

DAVID KAPRALIK: He would record in the studio that John Phillips had built. That was one of the attractions of the house, that Sly had his own studio. At that point, CBS had closed its Hollywood studios. They had terrible union problems because the same union with the recording artists were also the television men and most of them were grandfathered into the recording business. They were radio engineers that just couldn't relate to the kind of music they were being asked to record. Plus, the studios weren't equipped to record it. They were fine for Frank Sinatra, Tony Bennett, Barbra Streisand, and the big bands, but not for Black music like Sly would make. The CBS studio had acoustics. The kind of music that Sly was making, it was better if the studio was padded and you couldn't hear the actual sound of the room. Almost everything was plugged directly into the board, anyway. He rarely recorded anymore in a studio with people playing all together. There were lots of musicians around. Ike Turner, Bobby Womack, Billy Preston—these were the people who actually played on the records in some cases. They were there and he was recording and they were musicians, so there is a good chance they would add things.

JERRY MARTINI: Hidden sliding door, then you go upstairs. Ray Conniff's son, Jimmy Conniff, was the engineer and he was real good. He was called the king of splicers—he could splice better than anybody else. He had some real good engineers up there. But it took a long time to get anything done, for obvious reasons. He still turned out some pretty creative stuff. Herbie Hancock and Miles were hanging around, Johnny Watson. He had everybody. He had access to a lot of musicians. Cynthia and I played on everything, all the way through.

BOBBY WOMACK: He played on some of my stuff. As a matter of fact, a lot of my *Communication* album was cut at his house.

I played on *Riot*—I hear myself on that—and I probably played on a lot of other things. But you would come back and tapes had moved and no one had seen them but him. There was some shit that never came out. There were many nights that I didn't want to go home. I was just there and we just kept cutting. He'd say, "Bobby, you gotta sing on this, gotta do this." He was very creative, into that, and I was off into that whole trip. To be into that, you had to live it. There was a riot going on up at his house. You would be playing one minute, the next minute he would say, "Everybody better find a hiding spot because I am going to turn Gun loose." I say, "Who is Gun?" They say, "That is a pit bull and that motherfucking dog is crazy." I would run and hide. This dog don't play.

STEPHANI OWENS: Sly recorded all the time. He had to be in the studio all the time. A lot of money was spent in the studio, probably a lot of money wasted in the studio. He would go into the studio six o'clock one evening and be there for two days.

KITSAUN KING: They could be up there for days and people would even forget about them. Go up there and people were just laying out, high. Music was made, basically, in the middle of the night. Most studio sessions were overnight. Days on end. The longest time I stayed up without going to sleep was five days in a row when they were recording. It was done by drugs and other methods. Some things were recorded at the house in Bel Air, some at the original Record Plant. They did a lot of dope at the Record Plant. Sly would be totally high. He would be so high that he would sit with his guitar going over, going over, going over.

VERNON "MOOSE" CONSTAN: I didn't like to do the long stretches, the marathons. When I would come back up there after seeing him awake for three days, it wasn't any fun to talk to him because he didn't make much sense. Jimmy Ford was there, along with everybody else. Jimmy Ford was a White guy, of course, who never got any credit for anything.

ROBERT JOYCE: Occasionally, Sly would call me at four in the morning after he'd just stopped recording. He'd want to go for a drive. I would fire up the Bentley. He would get in the back. We would chat a little bit and I would drive around Beverly Hills and drop him off. I would sit outside for ten hours.

BOBBY WOMACK: He had these two big old peacocks, and if you came out of there at night fucked up, forget it. These two peacocks would attack you. You coming outta there and they just fly off the roof. Big old peacocks. These things would fly down on you. That would freak you out because you would come out of there totally spaced, saying where are these fucking peacocks, motherfucker, because you knew they were out there.

VERNON "MOOSE" CONSTAN: I lived there for about a year. Then it got too much like a prison. It was too regulated, like "Where are you going, what time are you going to be back?" It wasn't that way before; he was much more relaxed. He started getting paranoid. Coke, along with building up your ego, gives you a terrible fright of things that could happen, like the gates had to be closed because somebody was going to crawl over and shoot him.

ROBERT JOYCE: We used to call it the prison because we couldn't get off the hill. There were no clocks in the house. No clocks. Clocks were not allowed in the house. Sly's thing was no time. He made time, that was his thing. Now, we are doing it right now. That was the mentality.

JERRY MARTINI: He moved me down to the bottom of the pool house to this filthy mess where there were used tampons and shit. My wife fixed it up and sometimes when he wanted, he would give that cabin away so his friends could stay there.

KITSAUN KING: Freddie never really moved to L.A. He'd come down and stay, but he lived in Oakland. He would get away and dry out. He had a house in Oakland Hills, not too far from Rose's. That was where he lived. He would be in L.A. for periods of time, but he would be back. I'm sure he still did drugs, but he wasn't in the same kind of L.A. mish-mosh, that whole bizarre world down there. I don't think he did well with drugs. Also, I don't think he took the amount of drugs that Sly did.

Freddie was really great. He was a wonderful person, but [our relationship] was just drug-induced bizarreness. Fortunately, it didn't develop into anything. Freddie had the whole I'm-not-as-good-as-Sly thing going for himself. In the family, Sly was the god. Freddie always felt like the little brother, under Sly's shadow, that kind of thing. But Freddie had nothing that Sly had. He had no vision. He didn't have the same kinds of talents that Sly had. Not to say that he didn't have any talent. He was a good guitar player and a good singer and very sweet. But he didn't have the kind of artistic vision or drive that Sly had.

Freddie Stewart, 1970.

FREDDIE STEWART: I was always little brother. I fell into a thing where I relied upon him. When we first started and he said, "Come to San Francisco," I went. I kind of relied on him for whatever happened. I expected him to look out for me. I did think that he would always look out for me business-wise. I got into this thing of depending on him.

HAMP "BUBBA" BANKS: Freddie was a nuisance to Sly. He was just always there. He did not fit. He tried to, and I think he tried too hard. Freddie didn't say the right things. He was always the little smart aleck. He didn't know what to say, so saying something smart would compensate for being Sly's brother. Sly didn't care. He could play. He was talented. Had he been a guy that Sly called in and let him go home, he would have been cool. Like Larry, his best friend. Larry had his wife. All while they were in New York, while he was with Rose, Larry had Freddie's wife, Sharon, too. Freddie had a thousand-dollar phone bill at his home when he came back from all the calls from Larry.

STEPHANI OWENS: Freddie really idolized Sly. He was big brother. I think because of Sly, Freddie was exposed to a lot of things. He was very talented himself, but his talent was enhanced by the influence of his brother. It was a love/hate relationship. If Sly was finished with a woman, Freddie might try and latch onto that same person. It always seemed that Freddie always seemed to look up to his big brother. Somewhere along the line, their relationship deteriorated because Freddie didn't get the acknowledgment that he was looking for from his brother.

KEN ROBERTS: I took the two shows and they were sold out. I never did anything or even talked to Sly at that point. I made sure that I went on the planes he went on, etc., without talking to anybody. Then, a couple of months later, he had a few sporadic dates booked. Some he showed up for, others he didn't. It was in a lot of disarray. Al came to me again because he was trying to piece together some dates to help Sly with some money. He said, "Would you book some more?" We did three shows in Cherry Hill, New Jersey. Those three shows went pretty good. We added them all at the last minute.

HAMP "BUBBA" BANKS: He did Dick Cavett so bad. What happened is we went to Cherry Hill. This is where Ken Roberts came into the picture. He was the promoter. J.B. brought him in the room to meet Sly. Ken Roberts bought us all a portable television with AM/FM and cassette. After the show, David Kapralik took us to Muhammad Ali's house because he did some records on Muhammad. Ali's wife loved Sly. That night, after we left Ali's and went back to our hotels, Sly slipped out and went back to Los Angeles.

JAMES VERNON "J.B." BROWN: Just said, "We're going to L.A." We went from the airport to the house, then turned around and came back again. After many phone calls. If he didn't make *The Dick Cavett Show*, he was history. At least, that was the statement.

HAMP "BUBBA" BANKS: I called the next day and talked to him. Sly was saying, "Man, I will be there." Now I'm panicked.

Bobby Womack was there, so I told Bobby, "This man has to be on *The Dick Cavett Show*."

BOBBY WOMACK: He just found every excuse to not go on that show. He was petrified, now that I look back on it. He was scared to death. You would take him downstairs and he said, "I gotta go back upstairs." This went on for at least two hours.

HAMP "BUBBA" BANKS: Finally, the plane did get to New York, after they missed this one and that one. I didn't have time for them to get there, so I chartered a copter. Everything was ready. But I couldn't find Sly. He was in the bathroom, hid. I went in the bathroom and couldn't find him. Finally, I went back and looked up under the toilet door and Sly has got both feet up on the commode. He's kneeling down, snorting cocaine. I said, "Sly, you have to be at *The Dick Cavett Show*." He used to always go if he thought I was going to get mad at him. Now we were laughing. The helicopter was there. We went out there and he was stressed. It was a two-passenger helicopter, but he came with Bobby. I told Bobby to go with him. I got him on the helicopter and it took off. But in the car coming back to the terminal, I looked at the helicopter and it was coming back to land. We rushed to see what's wrong. They landed so him and Bobby Womack could change seats. Sly wanted to change seats because the wind was blowing his cocaine around. When I did reach the studio, Sly was still in the dressing room. They asked me to get him out. Dick Cavett went to commercial. Finally Sly came out and was walking down the stairs. Dick Cavett saw Sly and Sly looked out at him. Dick Cavett announced him. Sly looked at Dick Cavett, then at me, and said, "Bub, I got diarrhea, man, I gotta go back."

BOBBY WOMACK: Dick Cavett is saying, "I can't believe that you are going to do this to me—you got these people waiting, all you gotta do is walk out there." They were trying everything. We finally got him to go and get close to the stage and he says, "I got diarrhea, man, I gotta go to the bathroom."

GREGG ERRICO: There is a little spiral staircase from the green room. It is upstairs. It is tiny. We are on our way down. They called one minute. On our way down, about halfway, there is this little step-off into a bathroom. We're coming down and Sly steps off and he pulls everybody into the bathroom. Now it is less than a minute, forty seconds. He whips out a bag—Dick Cavett is calling us—and he proceeds to dip into it. We are hearing yells coming up—"He just announced you, you really screwed up, you're late, they are going to kick you off the show." So Cavett went to a commercial and he had announced us and we are in the bathroom. Then we went down and it was a good show. We kicked ass.

DAVID KAPRALIK: I was at the hotel on Sixth Avenue in New York, holding a press conference, turning on the television, and seeing a smashed Sly Stone on *Dick Cavett*. At that point, the dialogue between Sly and I had almost completely broken down.

JAMES VERNON "J.B." BROWN: I rented a helicopter because we had to go to Boston. Bobby Womack was flying in. The helicopter picked us up at the heliport and we flew to Boston. Sly had a violin case filled with drugs. He gets out of the helicopter and he hands the police his violin case. The police carry his violin case to the arena and say, "Here you are, Mr. Stone." I'm just rolling, 'cause if they'd only open that, he'd be so far in the jailhouse you couldn't even imagine it.

GREGG ERRICO: Everybody would call and say that he was messing with the drum machine and he wanted me to come down there. I'd get calls daily from him, from everybody, and I just didn't want no more part of it. I was done with it. It wasn't fun anymore. It wasn't giving me what I wanted, musically, to go out there and be on the road. Financially, we weren't making much money. The business was handled very poorly. I just had enough of it. More than that, I had seen that this wasn't going to work anymore. I took a look at the situation and I had a very strong sense, intuitively, what it can do, what it could do, or where it is going to go. I had seen the situation deteriorate and seen him not responding to it, refusing to respond to the needs of everybody on all different levels. He used to call up and say it would be better now. After a while, I wouldn't answer the calls. Then I made a decision, emotionally. I cut the umbilical cord. I was scared to even deal with it. Do you know what it is like to go on the road and try to play a gig and you know it ain't going to happen? You know you are going to have to go through this big scene and deal with all this craziness, this insanity. People were getting hurt. It got ugly within the group, around the group, the audience, the whole thing. People were doing goofy things, threatening each other. It wasn't comfortable. I didn't want to do it. I didn't want to be part of that.

JERRY MARTINI: Gerry Gibson only lasted a few months. He was the drummer for *The Banana Splits*, the cartoon. He's a Texas drummer who used parade marching sticks as drumsticks—they look like small baseball bats. He was a real mediocre drummer and was just at the right place at the right time.

STEPHANI OWENS: Sly in a lot of ways was afraid of himself. With all the intelligence he had and with his music, his being so in tune with it and how ahead of his time he was, there were very few people around him that understood where he was coming from. Gathering his old buddies around him was his way of keeping himself grounded, as opposed to dealing with the White man's world of record companies and presidents that didn't really have any feeling for where he came from and what he was all about. Sly had a tremendous need to be surrounded by people. I don't know if there were very many waking moments of his life that he spent alone. He always had somebody there, whether it was one of the guys, some of the guys, or a female. It was almost like he was afraid to spend time by himself.

JERRY MARTINI: That was the era that I call guns and dogs. It was a time that people were lurking around on the grounds and he sent his guards out to capture the guys and brought them in the house and interrogated them. They let them go eventually. It was an insane time. That's when Terry Melcher, Doris Day's son, sleazebag motherfucker, was around. I hate him, very bad person.

ROBERT JOYCE: Terry Melcher drove an old Mercedes general's car. He would come up to the house in that thing. Occasionally, we would go to his house where he had a lot of monkeys out in the back in the trees. He produced Paul Revere & the Raiders. He was Doris Day's son. He was a very strange individual. When they went down to his house, they would call me up. I was the home stereo man: "Take all the stuff over there, and set it up, because I am going to go over there tonight." Sly would come out and we would go. He would go over there and he would have an organ, plug it in. I would sit and wait. Two days later, he would come out.

DAVID KAPRALIK: Whenever I went to Hollywood, I stayed with Terry Melcher in Malibu. It was natural that when Sly came into my life, he was meeting some of my friends, and so he met Terry. They had a mutual interest in music. Terry invited Sly over to the house to play music. Sly was at the piano and Terry was standing next to him. Doris walked into the living room, on her way to her bedroom, and Terry introduced Sly to Doris. Then Sly started playing "Que Sera Será," and she sang along or hummed it along with him, said goodbye, and that was it.

STEPHEN PALEY: He was friends with Terry Melcher, who was a staff producer at Columbia Records. Sly collected old cars and either Terry or Doris had some old car that Sly was interested in. They went over to their house, just to check it out. Doris must have come out and they were introduced. He could be very charming when he wanted to be. He said to her how much he liked "Que Sera Será." That song was a huge hit for her in the fifties. In fact, it won an Academy Award. They went into the living room and Sly played and she sang it. They did a duet at the piano. Then, this rumor surfaced that they were having an affair. When it came out that he was recording this song, he didn't do anything to discourage this rumor, either. When asked about it, he would just kind of smile, but he wouldn't deny it. He wouldn't confirm it, either. She wasn't too pleased about this, needless to say.

Then he recorded the song. There was a rumor about her and Maury Wills, the Black shortstop from the Dodgers, so the idea of her fucking Sly wouldn't have been that outrageous. It had some credence. The very idea of Sly and Doris Day, bizarre as it seems, was grist for people and they kind of liked the rumor. It simply wasn't true, other than him playing with her on the piano. It was funny, Sly would act very strangely around other celebrities. I remember at Columbia studios, Jim Nabors was a Columbia artist, beautiful voice. He had a Rolls Royce and Jim Nabors was coming out of the studio and Sly was coming in and they stopped, froze, and looked at each other. Sly went over to Jim Nabors, shook his hand, and said, 'That is a beautiful car and you have a beautiful voice." Occasionally there could be a nice interchange like that, but you never knew how he was going to react. The fact that Sly even knew who he was surprised me.

JERRY MARTINI: Sly attracted everybody to the scene. Good people and bad people. Once you get involved in drugs, the negative people will always overshadow anything else, because cocaine is an evil drug. It brings you into all those coke dealers who will kill you for money, greed, or drugs. He had pounds of it in his safe. Seconal, Tuinals, Placidyls, 747s. There were reds. There were yellows. There were greens. You wake up, you take Placidyl, which he got from his doctor—it was a psychosedative. Then you snort enough cocaine until you can talk straight. It was like this up-and-down roller coaster. The whole thing was a nightmare until eventually I got back in my jeep, took my dog and my wife, and went back to my house. Left, no notice, and didn't talk to him for a couple of months. He was incapable of going on the road. Incapable of functioning as a traveling musician, doing what he could do so well.

KITSAUN KING: It was a first love for my sister, that kind of thing, as opposed to some high school boyfriend thing. I don't really know if you could say that the relationship was deteriorating. The people were deteriorating. It was more a question of Sly slowly melting down and becoming a completely bizarre person. My sister was very young, but this was not her idea of a way to live. That is for sure. We were exposed to musicians and that part of it, but this other stuff. I don't know if you could really characterize it in terms of a relationship deteriorating as much as people.

JERRY MARTINI: Debbie King, he threw her out. She was hemorrhaging, having some female problems. She was best friends with my second wife. Debbie stayed at my house and she was the sweetest thing in the world. I love Debbie. She is the nicest girl and he mistreated her. I think he was going for her sister Kitsaun, too, because he liked the sister thing.

STEPHANI OWENS: She was really into Sly's music and I think that she had a big influence on some of the music that he wrote. She may not say that. She was very young, eighteen at the time, and I think that she got thrown into an environment that was totally different than the environment in which she grew up. Sly could be very volatile at times, probably more from drugs then anything, but he was also the kind of person that wanted to run the show. He was the man. He liked to be in control, which I think all stems back to the pimp mentality, that he should be able to tell people, particularly females, what they should do. Debbie was not the kind of person that would just accept that.

JERRY MARTINI: Back then we were staying at the Holiday Inn on Fifty-second Street, where Freddie kicked the guy's ass. He did break the guy's jaw. The guy said something to Cynthia. Freddie just tagged the guy.

CYNTHIA ROBINSON: We just came into New York from the West. We put our stuff in the rooms at the Holiday Inn and then we were going straight to the studio. The guy taking our luggage into Rose's room said something. I told Freddie about it. Five or six hours later, me and Rose were going to go back to the hotel and bathe and change clothes because they were into the rhythm section at this point. When we went downstairs to get some cigarettes, I pointed him out to Freddie. Freddie starts talking to the guy and he walked off. The guy comes back with another huge guy. The guy tells Freddie to get up to his room before something else happens. The guy was walking towards Freddie. Freddie told him to not come any closer. Freddie hit the guy and was wearing this guy out. All of the sudden the back door opens and somebody tapped me on the shoulder and then hit me in the jaw. I grabbed a guy in the back of the neck and tried to hit him as hard as I could. I didn't know what was going on. I was being thrown down on the floor, somebody had hold of my legs. My face was in the carpet and I heard Freddie yell for them to get their hands off of me.

FREDDIE STEWART: Somebody disrespected Cynthia. I confronted the individual. Big guy, too. Said a bunch of words and called him out. He came at me and I kicked him. About four guys—the bellboys—jumped on me. They mopped up the floor with me really good. I didn't hurt so much. I'd been up and I was sort of high. One of the guys held me and another guy hit me. When it was over, they let me up. I went upstairs, got off the elevator, and called everybody—my brother, Bubba, my dad, the rest of the group. We went back downstairs and turned that place out. We just fought from the lobby all the way back to the kitchen. After it was over, we went right back upstairs. Few minutes later, we saw like maybe ten police cars out the window. They never came up.

KC STEWART: I remember the time in New York at the hotel with Cynthia, Freddie broke someone's jaw. And the police got there and said they were going to search their room, but they didn't have a warrant. So I told them to go ahead and get that warrant. And I told the band if they had anything in there to get it out. And the police never did come back.

NINE

SLY'S LAST CHANCE

David Kapralik, Sly, Madison Square Garden, 1974.

KEN ROBERTS: In July or August, Al had booked them on a few more dates. Sly asked Al, "Why don't you have Ken Roberts come with us?" I went with them to La Guardia Airport in their private plane. Sly showed up with his girlfriend at the time. I forget her name. As we were taking off, Sly had them stop the plane. He said, "I would like to speak with you." There were only four people—Al, myself, Sly, and the girl. He gets off the plane. I get out of the plane on the wing. He said, "You know, Ken, you have done three, four, five concerts with me. You seem to have a very even keel personality. I like you and everybody likes you. I would like to do some more things with you.

I like David, I trusted David when I first met him. He became our manager. I thought he was going to be awake in the day and asleep at night and I would be awake all night and sleep in the day and he wound up doing everything that I am doing. Some of the things I thought we were going to do, we couldn't do because we had legal disputes. Everybody seems to like you, so I would like to do more with you." Then he called Al and said, "Al, I would like to try and work out something between Kapralik and Ken." I'd known Kapralik. I met him a few times and he had liked me. I said, "Okay." I made a proposal to do more concerts. I became the exclusive concert promoter for Sly and the Family Stone. They weren't getting too many dates because he wasn't showing up, even though everybody wanted him. Between the arenas and the auditoriums and the colleges, he had canceled so many times, people didn't want to be bothered with him.

AL DEMARINO: When we needed someone to promote dates, to keep the cash flow going, and to help ease the tension within, Ken Roberts agreed to promote a number of dates, including three consecutive nights at Madison Square Garden, at which point we did not have any product out whatsoever. They had no product out for two years. For an act, in those days, to go into Madison Square Garden, very few acts would attempt that. It sold out for three nights. The other acts that were opening were Ruth Copeland, who was on Invictus Records out of Detroit, and a White rock act, Rare Earth, which was on Rare Earth, a Motown label—a White rock and roll night.

> From *Rolling Stone*, September 14,1971: "In the past two yews, Sly his managed to rack up the most erratic performance record since Judy Garland. According to his agent, he canceled twenty-six of the eighty engagements scheduled for him in 1970—twenty because his stomach was in convulsions and another six because of a clash until Kapralik. This year Sly has canceled twelve shows out of forty—ten because of a legal battle with Kapralik and two because his drummer quit. He has been late for two shows. As the cancellations mounted, Kapralik's slogan—"The Incredible and Unpredictable Sly Stone"—gradually lost its bright, euphemistic ring. Several weeks ago, Sly found out that no promoter in America would touch him. "Except," proclaims Kapralik, "the saint who came along, Ken Roberts." Ken Roberts booked Sly into Madison Square Garden three successive nights in the first week of September. It was Sly's last chance."

JERRY MARTINI: One time, we were outside in the limos and Sly was in the bathroom. We were waiting until the limousines overheated. We already missed one flight. We liked to go early to some jobs. Finally, Gregg and I had our limo. We said fuck this, let's go to the airport and get to Puerto Rico. Why are we waiting there for him while he is in the bathroom solving the problems of the world? We all know what that is about. So Gregg and I got there early. Later that night, there was a bang on my door and it was J.B. "Sly wants to see you, now." My wife was there. I didn't have my shirt on. He escorts me bare-chested down to Sly's room. Sly asked me why I left. I said that I was tired of waiting. We were out in the limousines for two hours. "Why didn't you just respect us and come out and do what you are supposed to do?" I asked. "Why do we have to sit out in the limousine for two hours sweating?" Sly looked at me and said, "You're dogs." He said he would "teach my ass." This is my best friend talking to me. He told me to get out. It was a situation that I never thought I would experience with him.

STEPHANI OWENS: He was a control freak. He liked to control the people around him. It didn't matter if it was his brother, another member of the band, a record producer, the president of the record company, or his manager, he wanted always to be in control. He would say things just to see what the effect would be. That's what the mind fuck was. He would say something to you and just to see how we would react to it. Most people would go along with his program. Very few people would say "You're fucked, too, Sly."

DAVID KAPRALIK: He started balking about recording, spending enormous amounts of time in the studio, refusing to give a finished record, finished product, and the first record that came out of this period was *Riot*. I remember creating a campaign that said "two and a half years is a short time to wait for a work of genius." That was to placate the record company.

LARRY GRAHAM: Basically, the *Riot* album [*There's a Riot Going On*] was, for the most part, overdubbed. For the most part, I would say that generally the other stuff was us playing together with some overdubs. But *Riot* was recorded a totally different way than we had recorded in that I didn't play anything, to my recollection, with the rest of the band. All of my stuff was overdubbed. If anybody else played with anybody else, I don't know. Maybe somebody else was there when they played. But for me, my stuff was definitely overdubbed. I didn't have a problem with that. I mean overdubbing as in playing my part along with the already existing tracks. And not necessarily what he would end up with was what I was playing, too. He was the leader of the group. Up to that point, we had experienced a lot of success, as far as having hit records. It wasn't the first time something had been overdubbed. "You Can Make It If You Try" is Sly on the bass. The concept of overdubbing was not foreign or strange to me. It was done on the *Riot* album to a greater degree than it had been done on any previous albums.

CYNTHIA ROBINSON: Larry was married to Gloria and they were kind of splitting up, so he was like super playboy. He was really pushing it, and during that particular album, Syl was trying to get the songs finished. He would say that we had a recording session and he wanted us down there at such and such time. We would get down there, but Larry would say that he was coming and wouldn't show. A week would pass and he'd finally show. I remember Sly himself doing the bass line to "(You Caught Me) Smilin'." He had that already done when Larry finally showed up after a week and a half. I was there when he kept calling and Larry didn't show. Sly went ahead and did the bass line because he had a deadline to meet.

STEPHEN PALEY: I didn't hear anything from *Riot* until it was turned in. I worked at the record company and I hadn't heard from him in like a year. When I finally heard it, I flipped, especially when I heard "Family Affair," because I knew that would sell the rest of it. I thought the rest of it was interesting. I love the song "Time." I love parts of "Space Cowboy." There are so many brilliant things on that album that I had never heard before and to me that is so rare, not to hear recycled stuff that other people have played. It was coming from a whole new place. You can hear the beginnings of it in the stuff he had produced for Atlantic. You could hear the beginnings of it in Little Sister, Joe Hicks. But it came full circle in *Riot*.

It was two years between *Riot* and *Stand!*, with only the *Greatest Hits*. Two very long years. In fact, David Kapralik came up with a slogan, which he forced on the company: "Two years is a short time to wait." He kept saying that and he had buttons printed, things like that. Not only did the Greatest Hits come out, but an album that is very important to Sly's career, in terms of breaking him to a wider audience, and that is the Woodstock album. I had something to do with that. Clive Davis didn't want to allow Atlantic to put Sly's performance on that album. He didn't want CBS artists appearing on other labels, especially Sly. Having Jerry Wexler and Clive Davis as friends of mine, I one day brought Clive out to Jerry's house to soften him up about allowing the track to appear on the Woodstock album because Clive was so adamant.

I knew "Family Affair" was going to be a hit, it was so unique and so melodic, just very special. I had never heard a record like it, exactly, with the strange vocal he had and the rhythm machine instead of the drums. That is Billy Preston playing on the electric piano. Sly is playing the chords, but he is playing the little licks. I just knew it was a hit and he didn't hear it. He wanted "Love N' Haight." Ron Alexenberg, who was head of promotion, and I decided to override Sly and put it out anyway. He couldn't do it because Sly had the rights to choose his own singles, so we made acetates and sent them to stations. I said, "Sly, I don't know how this happened, but they are playing the record—we have to go with 'Family Affair.'" He knew that it was probably my doing and he was annoyed. He said that it better be a hit. Not only was it a hit, it was the biggest hit he ever had. It was over two and a half million singles. It was a giant hit.

PAT RIZZO: I was playing in New York at July's Jazz Club and one of the guys traveling with Sly, J.R. Vatrano, was from New York. We went to school together, Bryan High School in Astoria. Originally, they wanted me to replace Jerry Martini. I stopped by his hotel on my way to work one night and auditioned for Sly in the bathroom. I got the gig and found out that Jerry decided to stay, and they decided to keep me in the band, too. Jilly Rizzo was kind of like an uncle. I introduced Sly to Sinatra at Jilly's one night.

JERRY MARTINI: The reason that Pat Rizzo was hired was because I got fed up with the fact that he wasn't paying us. I hired attorney George Davis two or three days before an important tour. All the managers, including Ken Roberts and David Kapralik, we were in Melvin Belli's office. I demanded all the money up front in escrow before I went out, and I got it. Shortly after that Pat Rizzo showed up in the wings and they let me know that if I ever did that again, I would have a replacement.

AL DEMARINO: Ken and I went to the same university. I did all my undergraduate work at Seton Hall University in South Orange, New Jersey. Ken was a couple of years ahead of me. I was doing radio work at the college-owned radio station, WSOU-FM, and Ken was the big man on campus because he was promoting concerts on campus. It was probably the best concert program, frankly, at that time in America. Then from booking college concerts at Seton Hall University and West Point, Ken became a commercial producer of concerts and, eventually, a manager. Ken has always been an astute promoter. Through me, number one, and also through his relationship with Peter Bennett, Ken was brought in to promote concerts more regularly—to help reduce the tension between Sly and David. But also we, obviously, were losing our reputation with key promoters. We needed to keep the band working and that is what we did with Ken. What we did is devise a formula where "D.K. concerts" became a reality and helped channel some money back to David and keep the band earning money also.

KEN ROBERTS: I looked at this like the Lloyd's of London theory—the higher the risk, the higher the reward. I said to David, "Right now, you are making 20 percent of nothing and William Morris is making 10 percent of nothing. If I put up the money for the auditoriums and the guarantees and all of that stuff, then I want a certain percentage of the gross of the concerts, because I am the one taking all the risk." I had to put up a lot of notary credits in case he did not show up. The band didn't have any money. I had to advance some of the money for the different people. Advance it to Sly, then he would give it to his musicians. I did everything through the proper channels. I put everything up. I would get my end from the top, and all the expenses would come out, and anything that was left would be Sly's and the group. And there would be a lot of money left. It was not that there was going to be nothing left.

The way I looked at it is that it was up to him. If he wants to spend it all on airplanes and instruments and all that, that is their problem. It has nothing to do with me. Prior to me being involved, because Kapralik had advanced all this money during the course of their time, part of the settlement was that every fourth concert that Sly would perform would be called a D.K. concert. Every fourth concert, all the money would go to Kapralik to pay back some of the money that he advanced. So, unfortunately, sometimes Sly would cancel that fourth concert and delay it. They had these fights, but they really liked each other. We did a whole series of concerts that year. Sly said, "You seem to be doing all the work—you are not only the concert promoter, you're basically my manager." Kapralik at that time was still in the adversarial position, yet they were friends.

JAMES VERNON "J.B." BROWN: I think that Dave Kapralik had gotten a little bit way out there. There was one incident where I had to go into a room and kick the door in to get Dave Kapralik because he had ODed on pills. We were in Florida and Dave Kapralik was laying in the bed naked. He had ODed or was trying to commit suicide because he was in love with Sly. At least that was what was coming out of his mouth.

DAVID KAPRALIK: I tried to kill myself several times. The intensity of my relationship with Sylvester Stewart and Sly Stone was unbearable for me, this disintegrating relationship. No one would touch Sly. My lawyer, Peter Bennett, had suggested I bring in Ken Roberts, who promoted Madison Square Garden and other gigs that were trouble but successful. I knew that if I continued, I would be dead. I turned over the management to him, so I could live. I had no choice but to die or make a paradigm shift. I recall going in on my knees before Sly, engulfed in tears, imploring him, begging him to let me go, so I could live. I was doing so much cocaine. I was in so much pain, confusion.

KEN ROBERTS: I brought Peter Bennett in to be the negotiator for the new album. Sly got the first contract of any artist ever to get a million-dollar advance on each album. At that time, he had a hit with "Family Affair." Peter Bennett was David's lawyer, but he was neutral in the sense that he was also my lawyer at the time. I didn't have any need for a lawyer because the only thing I was doing was the concerts. It was to everybody's best advantage that something could get worked out. I was the catalyst.

AL DEMARINO: If you want to know the truth, I think there was more of a problem with the publishing at that time, more than there was about commissions, per se. Sly felt uncomfortable with the publishing arrangement. He felt that he was losing ownership of some of his songs, and that was a real problem at that time. I know for a fact that on certain songs, Sly didn't have his 50 percent covered and it bothered him. It bothered him to the point where he didn't want to perform.

CLIVE DAVIS: I have private concerns if somebody is over an hour late for a meeting, much less miss a concert. His drug habits I never experienced firsthand. It wasn't a secret. You could read about it. But it wasn't only Sly. I'm not saying I had no idea who the drug users were at the time, but I never knew that Janis Joplin was doing anything besides drinking bourbon. We had a professional relationship and it just never became part of our dialogue.

STEPHEN PALEY: David told me something that I didn't know and that is that Clive was encouraging Sly to leave David because David was into drugs. I never knew this at the time and I thought that I was privy to everything. I didn't know that. I know there were new contracts written up and David was bought out, partly by the record company, major sums of money, hundreds of thousands of dollars to relinquish his share that Ken took over. There was a new recording contract in 1972. Sly's contract was completely renegotiated, and he got some big advance depending on the number of records that he sold before. If he sold a million records before *Riot*, he would get an advance on the next record of a million dollars when he turned in the tapes. Or if he sold five hundred thousand, he would get five hundred thousand dollars.

KEN ROBERTS: Sly wanted publishing on everything new. Everything that was old, Kapralik had a company called Daly City Music. Sly thought that he owned 50 percent of that. He found out that he didn't own any of it. That is what started these fights. He owned the writer's share and Kapralik owned the whole publishing. I had Peter Bennett become the lawyer and they set up two companies, one called Ili Ili—that was Kapralik's—and one called Fresh Productions, that was going to be Sly's. Kapralik would share in the producer's end of it, like he was, and he would share in the publishing, but half of it would be in Ili Ili and half of it would be in Fresh.

As time went on, I said to Kapralik that everything is moving in a direction where Sly is working. He has a new record contract, but I am basically doing your work. We made an agreement at that particular point, where he had another year to go on his management contract with Sly. Since I was doing all the work and he was still there, I said we will be co-managers. From this point on, until your contract ends, I want 50 percent of the management. And if I do take over the management of Sly after your contract is over, whatever time period you shared with me, I will give you 50 percent of my management fee for that same time period. That is the way it worked.

TEN

TIME TO GO

"Good Vibrations From Central Park."

KATHLEEN SILVA: I had an uncle who worked at A&M Records as an engineer. I was seventeen years old, modeling downtown as a fitting model, and I also had a clothing shop that I managed. One evening, I called my uncle and asked if there was any music. He said Billy Preston, Merry Clayton, and Sly Stone were going to be doing a jam. I brought my girlfriends and we went down. Billy Preston and Sly were wonderful together. Their music, like a puzzle, would fit together. It would be a whole sound that would float all through the room. I guess he had noticed me. I wasn't really paying attention. He invited my girlfriends up to Billy Preston's house, where they were going to have a party. I was with them and they were driving, which left me stranded. I was sort of trapped. I think he was just watching me—he was at a beautiful, white piano at Billy's house. There was no place to sit, so I was on the back of this couch, facing him. He was singing to me. But then as soon as I would assume that he was singing to me, he would turn around and look the other way. Sly said he would arrange to have me driven home, but his arrangement for driving me home was a thirty-six-foot Winnebago. The whole party went. He had me way in the back cabin, which is the master bedroom. He said, "I have to go home and get my driver's license."

We drove into this huge gate, 783 Bel Air, the same house they used in [TV's] *Dark Shadows*. As soon as you get into the gate, there was this cobblestone road and antique lanterns, like you were in old England. I looked out the window and I saw peacocks walking all over his garden. It was another world inside the gate. I went into the living room of this mansion and nobody was around. I saw this incredible couch. It looked like this bed a sheik would have. It had these low-roll arm things, huge, the size of a double bed, with a small back, all down feathers. This had already gone into the morning, so I was exhausted. I just figured that I would lay down and get some sleep. When I woke up, there was this guy staring at me. I said, "Who are you?"

"Sly told me to watch you," he said.

I ended up being stuck there for a while. I couldn't get a ride home and I wasn't allowed to use the phone. I wasn't being bothered. Nobody would come and try and have sex with me or anything like that. But I wasn't allowed to leave. Eventually, I ended up in his room. He had this waterbed in the center and I was looking at all of his monitors. He had cameras all over the mansion. I was just staring at the monitors and saw Sly singing and playing on his clavinet. Across the room, facing him, was Billy Preston playing on his keyboard and singing and they were making this fabulous music. I sort of dozed off and when I woke up, apparently they had gone to a recording studio, so I was all alone in the house. I called a cab and managed to find my way home to my apartment. That was our first meeting.

JAMES VERNON "J.B." BROWN: There was some bizarre shit going on. I remember Karen Carpenter going up to Sly and telling Sly that she loved him: "I love you, Sly." And Sly said, "Who is this bitch?" This was at the first American Music Awards. Dick Clark was panicking. "What am I going to do about Sly?" I said, "The hell if I know." He said, "He seems to be out of it." I said, "Yep, he's out of it." Dick Clark said, "You think Sly is going to come out?" I said, "Yeah, he'll come out." So he came out and he couldn't read his lines. We were out there going, "Sly, read the cue cards." Dick Clark's whole life was running past him. Sly was supposed to be the host, but by the time they got through editing it, you'd have thought he was a guest.

KEN ROBERTS: We were going to play Madison Square Garden on the Thursday, Friday, and Saturday. Then the Sunday afternoon, we were going to play the Spectrum in Philadelphia, which was a natural thing to do. Everybody liked him, he was showing up, he was playing, etc. He was fine. He was staying at the Hilton Hotel. The group was staying in a hotel in Soho. He was going to get up in the morning. Everybody was just going to drive down, very leisurely. Leave at twelve o'clock and he would get down there in two hours. The show was going to start at two-thirty. Earth, Wind & Fire was the opening act.

Twelve o'clock came, we were all set to go. He went out early in the morning. I was with him. We went to an electronics store at eleven o'clock that morning. He needed to get something for his tape machines. All set to go, ready to drive down, he got a tele-phone call that Larry Graham's girlfriend was sick. We go down to the hotel. Right in front of the hotel, five other limousines were all set to go. We got to the room. Larry's there, the girl is sick, uncon-scious. I tell him, "Everybody go down to Philadelphia, we will be there." Sly said, "We are not leaving until he goes."

It was getting at almost two o'clock. The show is starting at two-thirty. At night time, they had a football game or something in the big stadium next door. They wanted to get the people out of the concert at the Spectrum and get the people into the stadium. I had to call for helicopters. This is where all the money blew away. Where you could have had a nice limousine ride down for two hundred dollars, all of a sudden, I had to get seven helicopters. That is a pretty big job to do in fifteen minutes. But hell or high water, I am going to make him go. He is going to go.

They revived the girl, so I said, "Let's go now, she is okay. Have her mother stay with her." He said, "Okay, let's go." He figured I would solve the problem of him going. The end result is that I had to get six helicopters. We went to the helicopter port. We got on there, six helicopters, and flew across New Jersey. Sly, now, was tired. He got on the helicopter; it was me, the girl, and him. He fell asleep. When Sly would fall asleep, you would think he is dead. He would go into such a deep sleep that you could hit him, a bomb could go off, he would never move. Because he was up all night, he fell asleep when he got into that helicopter.

When we got near the Spectrum, I said, "Make sure the parking lot is open." It was just as if you saw a James Bond movie. These six helicopters come across, land right in the parking lot. Sly got off the helicopter, went in, and went right onto the stage at the exact time he should have gone on. Those are the things that happened during the course. He got on there like nobody ever knew all that went on. If somebody wasn't there to do all of that, to think of all of that, it would have been no show. That is what I got paid for.

ROBERT JOYCE: I did a makeup show at the Hollywood Race Track in Hollywood, Florida. Before I started working for him, they canceled a show there and the promoter was freaked. Lost his family, his wife left him—big stories like that. Real big problems. So we were going to do a job for him. I was called by Ken's office and told to rent all the equipment. They thought that the promoter was going to seize the gear from us. I got all the gear, showed up, and did the job. Some sheriffs showed up on stage, right at the end. By the time the group was doing "Higher," the crowd was whipped into a frenzy. No telling what was going to go on. The sheriffs came running on the stage. Sly was off the stage. They would always run to the cars and leave immediately. That was the program, everybody offstage and out of here. There was some sort of warrant or writ. They were impounding the equipment. They tried to hand it to me. I looked at the guy. I looked at Moose and

I went, "Let's get out of here." I climbed over some fence. We got some hippie chicks to give us a ride to the hotel. Got on the plane the next morning and split town.

JERRY MARTINI: One time we were playing in a big coliseum in New England and Sly was two hours late. Carmine Appice [drummer for Vanilla Fudge] was there. Pat Rizzo was there. The promoter was whining that he was ruined. Thirty or forty thousand kids were going to riot. The rest of the band thought, *Another one bites the dust.* Me and Rizzo said, "Let's throw a band together and have an opening act." I got Carmine, Timmy Bogert. I played keyboard. Carmine sang. We did "Superstition." We played for forty minutes, just jamming. They didn't love it, but they didn't kill us, either. They stopped rioting, Sly showed up, and we did the concert. The only thing that pissed me off was that nobody thanked me, except the promoter. I didn't get anything. They were tearing that place apart. The Family Stone could have gone on, but we didn't. They were real passive.

ROBERT JOYCE: At the Apollo, we had three shows: a Friday night, a Saturday night, and two shows on Sunday night. We got the Friday and Saturday shows off. Everybody loved us because we were working Madison Square Garden to twenty thousand and here we go to the Apollo, three thousand. This was a very special showing of Sly, basically. The whole band was at the Apollo, including Sly, but no Freddie. Oops. We wait and wait and wait. The crowd is starting to get restless. They are already in the house, sitting, waiting to go. No Freddie, no Freddie, no Freddie.

Sly comes up to me, honestly, probably an hour after we were supposed to be on stage. He hands me a small caliber pistol and says, "Take this with you. There is a car outside waiting for you, lay on the floor. We are taking you and Moose out of here." I know Freddie's not around. I know Freddie has been staying in New York for three or four days and that is bad news. We stayed at the Hilton Hotel. We had a floor all to ourselves. It was like *Romper Room*, going full steam. No Freddie. There is a black car in the alley. I'm laying on the floor and I poke my head up. The whole second show was lined up around the building waiting to get in. Sly knew this. Obviously, the promoter had come to him and told him, Look, not only is this crowd here, but the other crowd for the next show is here now. We got a problem. We never did that show.

HAMP "BUBBA" BANKS: Nowhere, not the Apollo, not anywhere, was special to Sly and the Family Stone. Freddie passed out at the Apollo. Freddie was gone. I think the thing was to see who could get the highest and be the most out of it. Freddie was always trying to get Sly's attention. Everybody was trying to out-high each other. That is what happened to Freddie.

FREDDIE STEWART: I don't remember that. I am not going to say that I wasn't. I might have been. I just don't remember. It is possible that I was.

JERRY MARTINI: The Apollo fiasco where we were sold out, on stage for the first show, Freddie was in a bad way. Freddie didn't want to play. He walked out. I wasn't there to see, but he couldn't play. He left. Sly canceled both shows and there was a riot. There was a line for two blocks. The house was packed. Sly was there. He was totally capable of playing. We didn't play the first show. We were on stage. Sly came out and said that we had to cancel because Freddie messed up. Freddie couldn't play. That is what killed us in

New York. Pat Rizzo had just joined the band. He didn't have a limo yet, but I had my limo, which got trashed. He had his little T-bird down the street and Pat and I could see the people jumping up and down on the hood of my limo. We went and got into his car. The word around New York was get Sly and the Family Stone. Our name was mud.

HAMP "BUBBA" BANKS: We were on Santa Monica Boulevard. He had a mobile home—a Winnebago. We had a driver, Anthony, and we were in the back, drugging it. Sly would never throw away no dope. When the police pulled us over, Sly got to milling around like nothing was happening. I said, "It is the police, man" and he just kept holding on to his dope. They were up front talking and Sly locked the door that comes to the back. I snatched the stuff out of his hands and pushed it down the toilet in there and flushed it. Needless to say, they spent two days cleaning the tank to get the drugs back. We all went to jail—me, Sly, J.B., Anthony, Kathy, April. April Silva is Kathy's sister and she was Sly's woman, too. Mine, too. I was Freddie—Freddie wasn't there. That was the first name that came out of my mouth—who is the dumbest sucker I could be? I was Freddie when they was booking me. I got bailed out as Freddie The two girls came and got us. We never went to court on that. That was dropped.

KATHLEEN SILVA: My sister happened to come and visit because she was a prodigy for golf. She didn't have a job. She was supposed to wake up at four in the morning, do her exercises, go out on the golf course, and that was her life. She was going to be a golf pro. When she came into town, she would stay at my apartment. I had called her because she was going to be in town and had no place to stay, and told her, "Sly says you can come up here and we can talk about what we are going to do." She came to visit for a while. She ended up going on her own. The world was very crazy, and at that time, she was only nineteen. We were both babies. She had no idea what was going on. That was not our lifestyle or our roles, so it was difficult for us. We were always trying to figure out things.

JAMES VERNON "J.B." BROWN: Kathy was with Isaac Hayes and left him. Her sister April ended up with Sly. They were both with Sly. They were both living in the same room with Sly for a long, long time, sleeping one on each side of him. They were just players. That's cool. They played him. He played them.

ROBERT JOYCE: We had more stereo gear than anybody on earth, period. Whenever we traveled, I could count on bringing home tons of stuff. He was in New York on Fifth Avenue, looking at all the newest and latest stereo gear. He was in this store in one of those lavish outfits he wore back then—a cowboy thing with holsters on this leather outfit. He started waving the dummy pistols around in the store. Some Arabian guy got all freaked out, thought they were real. He knew Sly was in the store. Got a little publicity for himself. Cops ran in and grabbed Sly. It was just a big joke and we did the show that night. It was just a day out on the streets of New York.

JAMES VERNON "J.B." BROWN: Larry was afraid. The whole situation was turning on him. Everybody. A lot of it was this shit with Freddie's wife. I think it was just the ego clash, too. I remember when I rode with him from Roanoke, Virginia, to South Carolina. It was one of them long, long rides with six limousines from one state to the next state. There we are, three to a limo cruising up the highway. I could tell it was coming at that time because Larry was in the car going, "This is not getting too cool." It was an unfriendly situation. Sly would say, "That Larry Graham." I think Sly really killed off the band. I think he figured that he could do it all anyway. He did, up to a point. No different than any other producer who does a certain amount of development of the tracks and the concept of the sound. I watched him on PCP. I watched him on cocaine. There was so much drugs that you can't fathom. He could have drugs all day long, all night long, for days, and still be doing his shit, still be wolfing down cocaine like it was going out of sight. Then, it evolved to PCP. I was not a PCP person. You would lose all perspective of how to control yourself. I was not one to lose my control. PCP was the beginning of his demise, when he started smoking those little cigarettes.

HAMP BUBBA" BANKS: I was the cat that fired Larry Graham. We were in New York City, getting ready to go to Madison Square Garden. Larry Graham had his whole little entourage and Sly hated this cat. I hated him, too. I called and said that it was time to be at the limousine. Now he's got his henchmen. Sly is no longer the only cat with the bad guy. He's got himself his own tough guy. I said, "Put Larry on the phone and tell him the car is waiting downstairs." He said, 'Tell everybody to go ahead." I said, "No, you are coming down now." I sent everybody else and stayed in his car. I was getting ready to intimidate now. I went in his room and his little henchman was walking around behind me. I decided to do something to him after the gig at Madison Square Garden.

KEN ROBERTS: We were playing Madison Square Garden and we were flying back to do a show in Los Angeles. I had to hire a jet in the middle of the night and get them back here. We flew back in the middle of the night. Al DeMarino had to help pack. Sly was sleeping, but we knew we had to catch the plane. We actually sacked Sly on a chair and had two guys carry the chair down the elevator and go through the lobby of the hotel, to the back entrance on Fifty-eighth Street. All the security guards were looking at this guy going out in a chair. They thought he was dead. The limousine was there and Sly had a plaid vest and black leather pants on. The guy stopped me at the door because they thought he was dead. We said he is sleeping. They said, "How do you know that he is sleeping?" "When he goes through this door, you will see that he is sleeping." Why? Because it is freezing. It was so cold, when the door opened, Sly went "whef." He just woke up. We pushed the chair and threw him into the car. We went to the plane back to California. The show was out at the L.A. Coliseum.

ROBERT JOYCE: We had an overnighter, Madison Square Garden to the L.A. Coliseum. We didn't know if we could get the equipment turned around fast enough. What we planned on using was all brand-new Acoustics, out of the box, delivered from the factory to the job. We had a private jet, so there was no room. We had a twenty-four-footer truck full of gear. All I would do was take the organs on the plane with me. No way we were going to get it done.

VERNON "MOOSE" CONSTAN: Everything was working good, but Sly was all screwed up. He could hardly walk. He was really fucked up on drugs. He got up on stage and he tried to play this Farfisa organ, a new one. He thought that it wasn't working. I don't know if it was really busted or not. So he made this announcement: "Moose, get out here and fix this organ—here is the guy, it's all his fault this is not working." I went out there and did something. I don't know if I really did anything, but I got it working. He went back out and played. He was mumbling and he was obviously too fucked up to be out there.

ROBERT JOYCE: There was some fucking major problems that night. Stevie Wonder opened the show and kicked our ass. Sly had to come out behind that. There was some technical difficulties. We got it licked in minutes. We had a bad show. Sly was getting booed. When Sly came offstage, he pointed his finger at me, indicating it was my fault. I said, "Hey, it wasn't my fault."

VERNON "MOOSE" CONSTAN: Sly came into my room. I was sitting on the bed. He said, "Why did you do this to me—give me the fucking organs that don't work?" I said, "There was nothing wrong." Boom, somebody kicked me in the head. They were all standing over me, like, do you want me to kill him? They did me in pretty good. I had cuts on my face. I was almost knocked unconscious on the first blow. They went through their karate shit and fucked me up a little bit, mainly to the head. I didn't have any broken ribs. I was sitting down, so I just fell back on the bed. I don't even know who it was. I never even saw the guy. He just kicked me from behind. They left. They took Rob's girlfriend. We were really worried about finding her because she was like kidnapped, didn't want to go with them. They took her. I got pretty tore up. I went to the hospital for a concussion.

EDWARD ELLIOTT ("EDDIE CHIN"): That was my party. Moose, he stole equipment or something. He tells me, "If you think I did it, do what you are going to do." I looked at Bub.

Bub looked at me and it was on. I was all over him like a cheap suit. Sly just...he wanted to be in it. After it was over, if I remember correctly, Sly might have went over there and did something. I don't know. To be in it; it wasn't natural for him.

ROBERT JOYCE: Knock on the door, a bunch of men come into the room, wail on me, and leave. Sly was in the room. Bubba was in the room. I couldn't believe I was getting whacked by him. That changed my life. A guy named Joe Hicks was in the room. I really can't remember what that was about. It was so traumatic. When they came in, Vern was in the room, too. It was our room.

That was a terrible thing to happen because I loved Sly. I would have done anything for him. I worked night and day. He was very uncomfortable about that. That really was what had to be. Because back then, things just had to be. Certain things had to be. That had to be. I challenged Sly in front of them. Right on stage in the Coliseum. Terrible night. I will tell you this, that night was based on PCP. Both guys were doing that. Acting all funny. It was new then. Moose quit and left. He never came back. That was his last night.

HAMP "BUBBA" BANKS: We get to Los Angeles. I call my man and tell him to meet me at the airport and bring a pistol. I had two dudes around me that, if they were here, you would feel uncomfortable. I was at all the wrong places for the right reasons. So he gets there and he is ready. Larry gets off and he has still got his little henchmen. Sly's got all his little flunkies and they is all doing the Sly-flunky thing. Larry has got all his flunkies and they is doing the Larry-flunky thing. He is matching Sly now. We go to the arena, flew right in. Everybody gets to their dressing room. I can't wait. My man is ready. They do the gig, but Larry smells a rat and they got out of there. But we all are staying down on Wilshire. The whole entourage is at the Cavalier—Jimmy Ford, Bobby Womack, everybody—because Sly is in L.A.

EDWARD ELLIOTT ("EDDIE CHIN"): We heard that Larry Graham had got a hit man to do Sly. Me and Bub come out of the streets and the Marine Corps. Hit man? This is getting good. We were in the lobby. We looked up and here comes Larry and some dudes down the stairs. I got behind the stairs, and when they came down, we worked them. We put the street on 'em. Their mouths got them in trouble. If somebody says that they are going to do you, that's serious. You don't joke certain things. If you say that you're going to do me, I'm going to do you first. You said that, so I believe that you meant that. That is what that was. We worked them so good. There was no getting away from us. We left some of them laying out.

HAMP "BUBBA" BANKS: Somebody tells me that Larry and his henchmen are in the lobby. I don't know why, but I had a walking cane in my hand. When I looked up, I'm in the lobby, and Larry's man is there. I took the walking cane and broke it over his head. We started whipping this cat so bad, I don't know if he was ever heard from again. But we whipped him so bad, Larry was able to escape. He got out of there quick. That's why I say I fired him. That was the end of Larry Graham.

PAT RIZZO: I was the one that got him and his girlfriend out of the hotel. That was fucking scary. I saved Larry's life. We did a show at the Coliseum and all the equipment was fucked up. The Hammond organ, everything. We went on to play, but everyone was pretty fucked up, especially Sly. We didn't even get through one song, I don't think. What flared up the hostility at the Cavalier, I don't know. I got him and [his girlfriend] Patryce out of the hotel room. I had a rented Ford Falcon. We got out of there just in the fucking nick of time. They were going to kill Larry. I don't know why.

LARRY GRAHAM: There comes a time when somebody leaves a family situation because it is time to go. It doesn't necessarily have to be because they are never going to come home again. It could just be time to go out and leave home. It became time for me to go. That is basically it. I didn't see a scene at the hotel. I heard about some negative things that went down, but I didn't see it. Actually, it was time to go overall. By that time, the changes that had taken place were already firmly established. Things were now the way they would be. It didn't look like it would be changing back to the way it was before. I was very comfortable, very satisfied with the way things were before, naturally hoping things would stay like that. But they didn't. It was time to go.

KEN ROBERTS: Something happened between him and Larry Graham. Had to do with a girl, something. I don't know what happened, really. Later that night, Hamp Banks and them went over to the hotel. They had a big fight or something and that was it. Larry never showed up again. I went up to San Francisco within the next couple of months and I met with Larry at his house. I met with Cynthia Robinson at her house. I met with Jerry Martini. We tried to get it all together. Larry said, "That is it." He drove me someplace. But when he got out of the house, as he stopped to get the car, he went and lifted up the hood. He thought there was a bomb. That is how frightened this guy was of this whole thing. He said, "I am never going back again." And he never did.

BOBBY WOMACK: When Larry left, I told [Sly] that I would go out and play bass until he got somebody. Now I was coming off two, three, or four hit singles in a row. It wasn't about ego; it was about "we-go." We were like that. I went through all the shit of getting on a plane, and he proceeds to interview bass players sitting at the studio listening to them play the music. I said, "What am I doing out here?" He said, "You're going to audition." He was a trip. He was Sly.

HAMP "BUBBA" BANKS: Now it kind of hurt a bit. They had a couple of gigs that they wanted to book and they didn't have a bass player. I told Sly that I would talk to this punk. I'll put him back if you need him. Sly and I went to this club in North Beach. Eddie Kendricks was there and he had a bass player named Wornell Jones. Larry was in the club when we went in there. He saw me and left outta there with his little people. I told Sly that I was going to talk to him. When Larry saw me, he dove in his car, peeled out, and left his people. I said, "Let me talk to you." He was in his white Cadillac. I walked alongside the car talking through a slit in the window. He said, "Give me a call, give me a call." That was it. No more Larry Graham from that point on. When I walked back in the club, Sly told me that Wornell Jones was the dude. He was there with Eddie Kendricks. I went to Las Vegas and got Wornell Jones off the stage before the next gig, put him in the limousine, and brought him back to Sly. Drove him in the limousine back to Los Angeles so Sly could meet with him. He might have done one gig.

RUSTY ALLEN: The first professional band that I got in, Johnny Talbot and De-Thangs, were playing at a club in Berkeley. Larry Graham came in, just listening. Larry told Sly—Jerry Martini told me this—that if he ever left the group, there is this kid he would want to take his place named Rusty. Time passed and I was over at Big Mama's [Alpha Stewart's] house and Sly called on the phone. He asked me if I could do this or I could do that. Naturally, I said yes. Next thing I know, I am in Virginia somewhere, me and this bass player that they were going to put in a Santa Claus suit, and Wornell Jones, who was playing bass for Eddie Kendricks at the time. We all played a couple of songs. On the gig. Not in a rehearsal soundstage, on the gig. Fifteen thousand people sitting out there. Incredible. Santa Claus went out there and played. Wornell played. I went out there and played "Sing a Simple Song," "Thank You," and "Higher." At that point, I remember Cynthia looking around and winking at me. At that point is when I got the gig. I never got the story on why Larry left—other than Sly was at odds with Larry and couldn't stand his guts. What the actual reasons were, I am sure he could tell you. I never found out. Never asked.

STEPHANI OWENS: That is when I left L.A. I got to the point where I had a cab come and get me. I packed a very small bag. I had no cash money. I had money coming from the union, but it wasn't there yet. I'd exhausted my bank account. I called Ken Roberts and told him that I had to get out of here. I had the cab take me to his house and he gave me two hundred dollars. I paid for the cab, bought a ticket, and never came back to even get the rest of my stuff. I had dissipated down to nothing, from no sleep, alcohol, and doing drugs. When I came home at the airport, my mother looked at me and started crying.

JAMES VERNON "J.B." BROWN: We had the fight in New York with Three Dog Night. I was invited to a party with Three Dog Night, so Sly says let's all go down. We went down to this hotel room, knocked on the door, and this guy gets out of line, so Sly smacked him. There we were fighting Three Dog Night. Well, it wasn't a fight. We beat them up. Me and Sly. Then we got sued. They sued me and Sly, but I never saw anything about it. I guess Ken Roberts handled it.

HAMP "BUBBA" BANKS: The police showed up at Bel Air and said they got a call that there was a dead body on the property. They started asking questions and I was the one that would intercept anything. That was my job. We did the whole little Eliot Ness act. They start searching and some of the police that came were mad at Sly already. They started combing the area, down at the pool house, the whole trip. It was really a huge place. The first thing that they came upon was the guns and they started spreading them out. Sly had bought a gun collection, I think, from one person. If you saw the guns laid out like they laid them out, you'd say, these cats are getting ready for war. All were different and unique guns which he never got back. At that point, the house was under police siege. They start coming out with drugs, bringing cases. The guns were already laying on the floor. They had to bring in a SWAT van to start hauling evidence because they were coming up with everything—drugs, guns, stolen this and that. Now we were under arrest.

Sly and I got bailed out together. I did a radio interview saying how they came in the house. They interviewed KC and he said they really messed him over, but he could have had something more to say, other than they wrinkled up his shirts. The guns that they acquired were a collection, I explained, and everything was unique. Hundreds of guns. Classics, collectors' items, antiques. I told them that all of the drugs were prescription drugs. It was true and that is why nothing ever happened.

When Sly went to trial, they were bringing all the drugs out and Sly was sitting in court sleeping. I took him to the bathroom. We walked out of the courtroom while the court was in session. He was in the shitter and I thought he was using it. I came back in a few minutes to check on him and he was in there snorting cocaine. He brought dope to court in Santa Monica. I said, "Sly, you can't do this." When the lawyer came in, he said, "Sly you can't do this." Sly said, "That's what I pay you for—so I can do this. If you're not the guy that can see to it that I do this, then I recommend you tell me who the guy is that I should be messing with, because obviously it is not you." We went to court and it got put off a few times. Nothing ever came of no court.

> From *New York Times*, September 28, 1973: "In Santa Monica, Calif., Sylvester (Sly) Stewart, of the Sly and the Family Stone rock group, was placed on a year's probation for possession of drugs. The 30-year-old Mr. Stewart will have to take part in a special program intended, according to state law, 'to give the experimental and accidental drug user a second chance.'"

ELEVEN

ONLY KIDDING

Sly and Kathleen Silva at their wedding, 1974.

KATHLEEN SILVA: I was constantly trying to get my little white picket fence. Why, I don't know. Obviously, I was young and I felt that I could change the world, but I didn't really decide to have my son because I thought it would change Sly's life. When I found out that I was pregnant, it was an exciting moment for me. Even alone, if I were to be alone, I was very happy and I wanted to have the baby. I think I didn't have any fear at all. Nothing bad ever happened to me, so I never really thought about the outcome. What if I am not in this world anymore? What if Sly and I never end up marrying? I never thought of things like that. He was always such a charming person and made you feel so comfortable that you never really worried about the outcome of anything until, there you are, out in the cold.

STEPHEN PALEY: The *Fresh* album was the first under the new contract and it was called Fresh Productions. David was gone and Sly was refreshed, so to speak. Sly rarely did drugs in front of me. I've seen him do cocaine a few times, but not very much. He may have been under the influence of it, but he never did that stuff in front of me. He knew that it would offend me. I can't be party to that. I knew there was a drug problem, but there was very little I could do about it. I never said, "Sly, don't do drugs." He would have laughed at me.

KATHLEEN SILVA: A lot of things that Sly used to do would end up in a song. People around him would end up being his new material for writing. It was amusement for him and I don't think that he meant to hurt anyone, but it was just that he found people and things fascinating. I remember one time when I was pregnant, and I was bitching at him because he was always going to the studio and doing things. He would be out all night and I would be home eating bonbons or cookies and milk. I wasn't with anyone and I felt left out. I used to wait for him and he would come home, be tired, and want to go to bed because he had been recording all night. I would be upset: "I don't like this." He made a song up: "If you want me to stay, I'll be around today, I'll be available…"

ROBERT JOYCE: *Fresh* was really his album. Sly was developing what he thought was the next stage in music. We were leaders in the field of what we were doing. The pressure all fell back on him to keep it going. Keep it going. Keep everybody paid, keep everybody going.

TOM FLYE: Sly was working on the *Fresh* album. It was pretty much done, but he wasn't satisfied with it and Tom Donahue suggested that he come see me. He booked a day at the Record Plant in Sausalito, came up from L.A., big entourage, and had an engineer with him. I went in the control room and the engineer was sitting in the back of the control room and I was sitting on the floor, on a step, listening to what he was doing. Sounded really good to me, really funky. This went on for twenty minutes or so. Sly said, "Somebody get up here and help me." I didn't know exactly what to do because he brought an engineer with him and this guy wasn't moving, but I got up and put up a multitrack and started going through it. That week we re-recorded about 90 percent of that record and mixed it. He played all the parts, except for the horns and stuff. If somebody else could play it better, he would let them do it. If not, he just played it himself.

CYNTHIA ROBINSON: He played bass more than he played drums. When you're playing drums, you have to keep that beat all the time and you can't slow down or speed up in a part. When you don't play all the time, your arms get tired and you slow down and he didn't want that to happen. He wanted to use a drummer to play his idea for him. He didn't have time to get his drum chops going. His ideas were there. He could do whatever lick he wanted. He could do it where other drummers could not. We were in the studio with that drum thing in "In Time," which is a backward funk thing. Every drummer who heard he was having a session dropped in. Sly wanted to see if any of these drummers could do it. Andy Newmark walked in on that session after five or six drummers came through—Buddy Miles, some others. Syl would show them the lick, how he wanted it done, and they would try and couldn't get it. Soon as he'd see a drummer walk into the studio, he'd be working on a song and stop to see if they could play this lick. Then Andy showed up. So he played it for Andy—I was there—and Andy sat at the drums and did it.

PAT RIZZO: I played the solo on "In Time." He would lay a rhythm track down and then start figuring out what he was going to do with the bass lines, guitar parts. I think he played most of the instruments. He always put the drums on last. He had the girls dancing in front of Andy Newmark when he put the drums on. That's why it's so difficult to understand the drum machine and what Newmark's doing on "It's Time." We finished the album in Sausalito. I lived in the hotel. Quite a few months, too. We were recording just about every day, sometimes straight through the night or a couple of days straight. Not that I did horns every day.

STEPHEN PALEY: I came out there and worked on it a little bit, but I don't remember too much about it. I just remember a lot of piecemeal recording going on. More micro editions. He completely let me do the cover. I got Richard Avedon to shoot it. Sly respected brand names and Richard Avedon was a brand name and the company was willing to pay what he wanted, which was a lot. *Rolling Stone* ran an item about the cover saying that Sly wasn't really jumping, he was standing on Plexiglas or suspended by wires. That is nonsense. He was absolutely jumping. He was taking karate. I wrote a letter to the editor. Another thing I had to write a letter about was when Clive Davis got fired. Some idiot at CBS Inc., not Columbia Records, issued a release that mistakenly identified an indicted heroin trafficker, a man called Pasquale Falcone, as Sly's manager. Sly had enough bad press without being involved, mistakenly, with an indicted heroin trafficker.

RUSTY ALLEN: From the time that I came in, after Virginia and the audition, the gigs were happening. Every weekend, Thursday night, early Friday morning till Sunday evening, I was parking my car at the airport and we were rolling. I mean every weekend for a year or something. I was thinking this shit would never end. This was when *Fresh* was starting to come out [1973]. It was cool. Then stuff started going down. I can't really put my finger on it because I didn't ask many questions. I wasn't but nineteen when I got into the band. I was just trying to make the grade musically. I was gigging with somebody I idolized. I was surprised that he didn't give his music more respect, from the standpoint of rehearsals. I was given a song list—learn these songs and, boom, hit it. A lot of times we pulled off gigs. Sometimes they were extraordinarily good. I remember in Ohio, on the Ohio Players' turf, they opened the show for us. Sly came in the dressing room and got us all together and said, "You guys know what you gotta do." That was all that needed to be said. But he surprised me that he didn't give his music the respect I thought he would.

Sly, "Good Vibrations..."

HAMP "BUBBA" BANKS: We weren't even there when we got evicted from 783 Bel Air. We were on the road and we got a message that we had to move out all the stuff. We panicked because we had a bunch of guns and stuff that we didn't want them to find if they were going to evict us. It was J.R. Vatrano's brother, Nicky—J.R. was on the road with us. Nicky was left there with no money. If you wasn't next to Sly, you lived under some buzzard conditions. You were waiting on something to die, so you could swoop down on it. You never were secure, ever. Anyway, I left one of my people there with Nicky, who was Sly's people through J.R. The two of them took everything they could. They were maintaining the property. They had to take my buddy's car, load up whatever they could from the property, make their way back to San Francisco with everything.

JERRY MARTINI: J.R. was going for a ride on my motorcycle. The throttle would stick. Half hour goes by and I didn't see him. The hospital calls. Throttle was stuck and he was driving too fast and ran into a wall on my bike. J.R. was in a full-body cast. His whole family came and stole him out of the hospital in a full-body cast. It was like a comedy. They stuck him in the station wagon and took him.

STEPHANI OWENS: He went into the hospital under an assumed name. Their dad and both of these brothers were a part of some Mafia something. J.R. was living under a different name. He had a real name and then he had another name. When he went into the hospital, we didn't even know how to find him. Kitsaun and I took him books and went to talk with him. Like one of those things you hear about but never see, in the middle of the night they took him out of the hospital in a body cast and shipped him back to the East Coast and we never heard from him again. That was the end of J.R.

HAMP "BUBBA" BANKS: We had a place at 25 Central Park West. Geraldo Rivera used to kiss my ass every day at Central Park West. He just wanted to talk to Sly. Melvin Van Peebles, Miles Davis, we were all in there shooting the shit. We knocked a wall out and put a studio in there. Sly had a room, I had a room, and a living room, and somewhere to use as a studio—that was all we cared about. One week, I didn't go to New York and Sly took Tom Donahue. I came to New York later, after Tom Donahue used my room. It reminded me of the three bears. When I got back, my little room, every chair was splintered. My bed was a palette. He tore it up. He was a big bopper.

Sly, Central Park West apartment, 1973.

STEPHANIE OWENS: After we lived in Los Angeles, we got an apartment in New York at 25 Central Park West. It was like a two-bedroom house. Rose and Bubba had a room right next to Sly's room and there was a living room. We would come back to the apartment and Rose would go to her room. Miles Davis or whoever was in New York that wanted to spend time with Sly would come by and stay up all night, doing drugs, playing music. Miles would come with his trumpet and they would sit and play on top of tracks. Or they spent time at the studio. KC would be there. He could stay there at the apartment, but he had another apartment in that same building. KC would come in and cook dinner for us in this closet kitchen. He always made sure that we ate good. That is one thing about Daddy KC. He would feed us and then he'd leave. He knew that there were drugs around, he had to have known, but nobody ever talked about it around him. Nobody ever did it in front of him.

HAMP "BUBBA" BANKS: We were in Ontario, Canada, in the dressing room, and he's in there and his dad is trying to follow him, trying to be part of the gang. Sly goes into the bathroom. His dad comes in there and Sly has cocaine. I said, "Sly, that is your dad." Sly said, "Dad, get out of here, man." Sly had his vial of cocaine and kept saying, "Dad, I'm telling you, this is cocaine—get out of here." His dad just stood there, pleading with him. "Me and Bub are going to snort this cocaine," he said. And he took his cocaine while his dad was still standing there and snorted it. His daddy looked hurt, but he still wanted to tag along and be Dad. He didn't know that Freddie and Cynthia were in the room every day. He had to go wake him up and help them dress, but he didn't know that they were doing anything. Nobody knew anything. He was just there. If Sly was in this bed with a broad and I was in the other bed, he would step over Sly to tell me, "This don't look right." They never blamed him for anything.

STEPHEN PALEY: Being friends with Sly and working with him, you could get a call at four o'clock in the morning and you would think nothing of that because he had a different clock than you or I. It was funny going over to his apartment sometimes. He lived in the Century apartment building on Sixty-second Street and Central Park West in a converted dentist's office on the ground floor. It is a big twin tower, art deco building. Ken Roberts lived in there; I think that is why Sly lived in there. I remember going over there at ten o'clock in the morning, and he was wearing jeans and a T-shirt and making corn flakes and milk. You don't think of Sly as being so normal and emptying ashtrays, cleaning the place up himself. He had that side to him. He could be very sweet, too.

TOM FLYE: He had a little sixteen-track studio in his apartment in New York. We would just use the stereo as the monitor system and had a mixer and an MM-1000 sixteen-track machine, a couple of mikes. At that point, his house in Bel Air had a full, competent studio hidden in the attic. Although the board never worked very well, I got some mike mixers and had a sixteen-track machine and we would record up there. It had a sliding bookcase that you would slide across into the hall and then there was a hidden staircase up to the attic where the studio was. We worked in Sausalito quite a bit. And then, from time to time, we would take one of my portable rigs over to his mother's house over by Stonestown. We would work in the basement there. He had a sixteen-track machine there, so the machine just sat there and I would bring the portable board and we would just use the stereo as our monitor.

He had a Toyota station wagon that was his tape vault and at the beginning of the session this station wagon would arrive and all this tape would be unloaded and dumped into a big pile on the floor. Then, at the end of the session, whenever that was, a couple guys would start picking up this pile, load it into the station wagon, and off they'd go. A station wagon pretty much full, I would say, forty to a hundred reels of tape.

He was always supposed to be doing an album. In a way, he was. He wouldn't sit and work on a track until it was finished. It was more spontaneous than that. A typical session would be, come in, get everything working. Of course, every time these tapes were given back to me, all the track sheets and all that stuff was missing. Finally, it boiled down to, put a tape up, and run when you heard music, and start bringing faders up. If it sounded good, you left the fader up. If it didn't sound good, you turned it off. Every time I would get the tapes, I would write out new track sheets and make all these notes, trying to get all this stuff organized. You could get it all up, then he would say, "I want to do a bass part." You would hook up a bass and do a bass part. Or he didn't have an idea right then. Then we would put up another song. Sometimes, he'd work a little bit on each one of them when they were put up. Sometimes, he could go through ten or fifteen tracks before he found something that he wanted to work on. Or sometimes, he would sit there and listen all night, make copies, rough mixes, stuff like that.

STEPHEN PALEY: He would book studios and not show up. It was just such a waste of time that I talked to one of the Columbia engineering people; let's just bring a machine to his house and send men over. He is paying for the time anyway, so it will be easier than blocking up a studio. They brought a big sixteen-track machine to Sly's apartment on Central Park West and set it up there. So we had a little studio in his house. The Columbia union engineers would just go over there, in shifts, rather than be at his beck and call. It was more efficient to do that than to have him tie up a studio that other people wanted. Sly wouldn't work like that. Pizza, sushi—he loved sushi—and the food. Then there would be smoking and there would be talking and there would be horsing around and every now and then they would get to work. Sly would lay down a bass part, a guitar part, something. You never really heard a finished song until much later. It was almost like needlepoint. Sometimes Miles Davis would be around. In New York, I remember that Miles loved Sly's work and was hanging around. He wouldn't play on it, he would just listen.

RUSTY ALLEN: One night, Miles came to the studio at CBS in New York. Me and Freddie went to Miles' place first. Then Miles came to Sly's apartment at Central Park West, went into the studio, got on Sly's organ, and started to voice these nine-note ethereal crazy chords. Sly was way back in the bedroom and he came out yelling, "Who in the fuck is doing that on my organ?" He came in and saw. "Miles, get your motherfucking ass out," he said. "Don't ever play that voodoo shit here. Get the fuck out." Miles left and I said, "Sly, that was Miles Davis you was talking to." "I don't give a fuck," he said, "playing that shit on my organ."

HAMP "BUBBA" BANKS: Miles didn't care. Miles was back the next day.

STEPHEN PALEY: Of course, the main problem was that Sly lost his perspective. He didn't know what was good and what wasn't good anymore. He erased wonderful things and rerecorded over them things that were not so good. He had a fear of completion.

He was afraid to finish anything. He kept thinking that he would make it better, but sometimes he would make it worse. Often he would. He lost his perspective and I think that was a direct result of the cocaine. He didn't know what was good and what was bad. I have "Que Sera, Será" in a completely different version. "Hobo Ken," a song about Ken Roberts, I suspect, I have a wonderful version that was completely abandoned that could have been a single hit. What he put out is far from this early track. Then I have some stuff that you wouldn't believe is Sly, some really mellow kind of jazzy things.

I did stuff for Sly that I've never done for any other artist. I had a shrink that I used to go to, a woman named Mildred Newman. She had a lot of famous people that she treated: Neil Simon, Paula Prentiss, many famous patients. She knows how to deal with people who have problems dealing with their success. So I took Sly with me once on one of my sessions and let him talk, thinking that this could help him because she is used to dealing with celebrities and, at the time, he was one of the first order. It didn't work. He liked her and they liked each other, but he never went back. I actually gave him one of my sessions as a present.

RUSTY ALLEN: We were in some obscure town down south and I had a sack. It was the worst. It was garbage. I was concerned about Sly. I went to his room and said, "Sly, look at this shit—this shit is garbage. I'm going to flush this shit. You don't want this shit, do you?" He said, "Yeah, man, let me have it."

STEPHEN PALEY: I just think he was a pig about it. He just couldn't get enough, he wanted it all. He didn't want to sleep. He just wanted to do cocaine constantly. He just had no moderation. He had taste as a musician, yet he didn't have taste in the way that he lived. He had such impeccable taste as a musician, as an arranger. He was a very nice person, too.

One time, he wanted to book time in a studio in San Francisco on Saturday morning at eight o'clock in the morning. I said okay. It wasn't easy to do, because it was people's day off, but I did. CBS had a studio on Folsom Street. At about eleven o'clock, I went there to see what was going on and Sly was fast asleep on the console and the engineers were just sitting there. I woke him up. "What the fuck are you doing? I went to a lot of trouble to book this for you. You said you had to have it and I did it. What are you doing? Why do you have to pay three hundred dollars an hour to sleep in the fucking control room? This is outrageous," He said to me something that I have never forgot: "Kiss the blackest part of my ass." I had to laugh. I said, "Sly, that is it. I'm going home. As for you people, the session is over. If you want to stay here, bill him because you are not billing us." I canceled the session and went back to New York. I was mad at him for about two weeks, I wouldn't take his calls. That was the limit. I went to such trouble to get him in at eight o'clock on a Saturday morning and then he just goes to sleep in the goddamned control room.

HAMP "BUBBA" BANKS: When they weren't working, I took Little Sister along with Freddie, Rose, and Cynthia and booked them as Sly's Family Stone, hoping that anybody that read it would just see "Sly" and "Family Stone," not the apostrophe. J.B. was one of the promoters of the concert. He called me in and I asked him to do me a favor. When I did get there, Billy Preston was there also. We headlined with a makeshift group. We pulled it off. The other promoters gave me a check that bounced. I put the group back on the plane and sent them back to Oakland. Then I went to get the money. When I got into this meeting about the money, they talked crazy to me. I got on the phone to New York, to people that I knew, and told them I am having a problem, put somebody on the plane. Bam, the money came right up. I went to the bank with all the parties involved, cashed it, and came on back home. They got a payday, which was all I was trying to do. I got nothing for that. I just did it because I felt responsible.

JAMES VERNON "J.B." BROWN: I ended up coordinating the Edmonton International Pop Festival, which was taking place in Alberta, Canada. Sly and Ken Roberts didn't want to do it. So Bubba said, "We'll bring Rose and the Family Stone up." We had a host of acts, Buddy Miles, Joan Baez. I ended up finding out that I was dealing with some Mafioso kind of group. They didn't want to pay the Family Stone. Bubba and I were up in this suite and they were threatening to throw us out the window and we were threatening to throw them out the window. Bubba said, "Let me make some calls." He made like he was calling the mob. They gave him the money.

KATHLEEN SILVA: I cried one day. I told him my son is going to grow up and go to school and he is not going to have a real man, a family man, and I want to leave you because of that. If I am going to be living with you, my son is going to be considered a bastard child, not having a proper family name. This is not the sixties anymore and we are in the limelight since you are in the limelight. I might as well go and get my own place to live on my own with my son. It would be the same, wouldn't it? We'll just see each other. He didn't like that. He said we should get married. He said he loved me. He always said he loved me. I think he really did want that kind of a world that was a special world, part of a world that he wanted. He admired his mother and father being together all those years, his sisters' families and stuff. Unfortunately, I don't know how to explain that part of it. Kind of crazy.

HAMP "BUBBA" BANKS: She was a pretty girl, but she was a straight airhead. She had illusions of being an actress. I think her mama was in *Planet of the Apes* or some shit. I think he was trying to have a responsible image. I think Ken Roberts might have coaxed him into that. The day we went down to City Hall in New York to get the license, him and her were fighting. It never was a marriage per se—"I love you." It wasn't that.

Sly and Kathleen Silva at their wedding.

STEPHEN PALEY: Sly called me up once and said that he was playing Madison Square Garden and he was going to get married, too. And I said, as a joke, "Why don't you get married as your first act?" Sly laughed, then called me back and said that he was going to do that. That it was a good idea. I told Sly that I was only kidding. I didn't mean it for real. It is a tacky thing to get married on stage. Then I thought, maybe you can, as long as it is done well. I got Halston involved—he was the biggest thing, he was like Armani now—to do the wedding clothes for free. All we had to do is pay for the materials. He knew that there would be publicity. Bobby Zarem, who worked for Rogers and Cowan, had just done the publicity for Cybill Shepherd's record, which was horrible. But it was getting so much ink that I wondered, if he could do this with Cybill Shepherd, what could he do with an artist that had hit records? I knew Bobby, slightly, and I liked him. I went to Irwin Sieglestein, who was then running the company. I said, "Sly is getting married, can I have a budget for a party?" He gave me twenty-five thousand for the party and I gave five of it to Bobby Zarem, and twenty thousand to the Waldorf-Astoria.

I decided that we wanted to play "Family Affair" instead of the wedding march. I asked Sly to record us an instrumental version. I tried to book the studio, but it had been reserved by John Hammond, the most respected A&R man of all time whose career ranges from Bessie Smith to Billie Holiday, Benny Goodman to Aretha Franklin, Bob Dylan to Bruce Springsteen. This is a man who is formidable, but I told him that we really needed it because of the deadline. I asked him if he would like to produce the session and John was delighted.

The session was booked, and I don't remember if Sly started and didn't finish or kept John waiting. It was good enough so we could use part of it and then mix it in with MFSB, some group that did an instrumental version of "Family Affair." I used a combination of the two and I made it work for the concert. I wasn't going to allow Sly to fuck over John Hammond. I liked John and John was kind enough to relinquish the time that he had booked. I could pretty much get Sly to do what I needed him to do. I felt like a lion tamer with a chair and a whip. I would go in there and Sly was like this ferocious lion that I could train for the most part. But every now and then, I had to crack the whip and hold the chair up. It was very much of a lion tamer-lion relationship. But you have to like the lion; otherwise, you couldn't do it. If you hate the lion, it would be a very ugly scene.

HAMP "BUBBA" BANKS: Steve Paley was his best man and that bothered me. If Freddie hadn't done it, I would have. Everything he did bothered Freddie. Freddie was not something that Sly was proud of. The whole thing lacked respect. Nobody respected nobody. Mine, I didn't worry about. I demanded mine. I didn't care what you thought of me. Steve Paley was a power move by Sly and Steve Paley was the nicest cat you would ever want to meet.

STEPHEN PALEY: Probably the greatest gesture he ever paid me as a friend was asking me to be his best man at his wedding, which really pissed off his brother, Freddie. His mother asked me to say I wouldn't do it. I said I won't do that. It was up to Sly. I won't insult Sly by turning him down.

JERRY MARTINI: Everything was orchestrated. Don Cornelius, Geraldo Rivera were ushers. Andy Warhol was there. The whole New York gang was there. The party was at the Waldorf-Astoria. I came in there with a blonde on each arm. Drunken fool. We wouldn't have sold out if Sly didn't get married. It was an extravaganza. I looked pretty good. I wasn't all drugged out. I sure was later that night. I remember being cognizant. But it was a joke. Never in a million years could I see that relationship happening.

STEPHEN PALEY: I got in a huge fight with Ken Roberts over the wedding. "If we are going to do this, Ken, we can't advertise because it is tacky, it is embarrassing, you can't say 'wedding on stage'—people will know because it will be leaked." It will be a surprise, a surprise that everybody knows. I hit the roof. "Wedding on stage"—that is so tacky. It embarrassed me and I made him back down.

RUSTY ALLEN: We must have had twenty limousines. Fashion models were holding gold-sprayed palm leaves. Fifteen-hundred-dollar Halston outfits for each band member. Waldorf-Astoria. Killer. You can't really fathom how deep that shit was. Then he has a full house at Madison Square Garden, saying "I do." I don't know if it was a gimmick to sell out the gig or what. Whatever it was, it worked.

FREDDIE STEWART: I didn't really look at Kathy thinking she was going to be Mrs. Stewart forever and always. I didn't look at it like that because I wasn't even true to my wife. I didn't look at her like she was going to be gone tomorrow, either. I just didn't look at it.

STEPHEN PALEY: The night of the wedding, Maureen Orth, who was a writer for *Newsweek* at the time, Sly tried to seduce her in the very next room, literally, on his wedding night. The two journalists that I gave access to were George Trow from *The New Yorker* and Maureen Orth. They, pretty much, could come and go as they liked. I gave them exclusive access because I admired their work. Both of them wrote nice pieces. George's piece was like seven thousand words, and *The New Yorker* liked it so much that they put a full-page ad in the *New York Times* to advertise it.

The party was fun. I knew a lot of social people in New York and invited a lot of them to the party, even the ones that didn't know Sly, and they came because it was a fun event. We publicized it as being a real event. John John and Caroline [Kennedy] came. It reinvigorated his career and if only he had the product to follow it up, it would have made him a big star again, as big as he was during the Woodstock time. But *Small Talk* wasn't a good album. It was really third-grade Sly. It came out at the same time [1974]. It sucked. The single ["Time For Livin'"] was no good. It started off good. It was the best that was on there and you make the best with what you've got.

It was all my idea. It was all free publicity and it got three pages in *Time* and *Newsweek* in color. It got front page of the *Daily News*, the *New York Post*. *The New York Times* carried it. It was on the Cronkite news, the Brinkley news. It got every kind of publicity you could get and the record didn't sell one more copy than it would have. The people that were exposed to the publicity were not the people that bought Sly's records. Had Ken Roberts been David Kapralik, he would have known how to market Sly. The most that we could do was when Sly cohosted *The Mike Douglas Show* afterwards. He got to the point where he was big enough to do that. They never followed through and I left the record company after that time.

HAMP "BUBBA" BANKS: When he got married, I was mad at him. I should have been his best man. Automatically. When I married Lillian Scott in 1964 at Saint Dominic's, Sly was my best man. He flew in from some gig in Texas to be there. Around the time he got married at Madison Square Garden, Rose and I got married, too. We were in Las Vegas for a gig and Rose and I ran off and got married before Sly and I had to fly back to New York for some reason and leave her there.

KATHLEEN SILVA: My son is named Sylvester Bubb Ali Stewart. Bubba was Sly's best friend and Ali was to be Sylvester's godfather. Sly loved and admired Muhammad Ali and Muhammad Ali liked Sly, too, as a friend. They may not have gotten along when they both appeared on *The Mike Douglas Show*, but what you didn't see was Muhammad Ali hitting on me pretty hard back-stage in front of Sly: "What are you doing with that fool? Come on over and be with me." Muhammad Ali, I think, always had a fancy for Polynesian girls, especially the native-looking Polynesian girls. Poor Mike Douglas tried to keep that thing: "C'mon, let's all get along." Actually, Sly, I think, handled it well. He tried to let that be a good show and was still very humorous and kind about it. But Muhammad was very egotistical and rude.

HAMP "BUBBA" BANKS: It happened in the dressing room before the show. Sly said something like, "Here, meet my wife." And Ali said, "You couldn't do no better than that?" Sly said, "Who you judgin' by—that Amazon you got?" When he came on the show, Sly stood up and said, "I love Muhammad Ali," and Ali walked right past him.

JERRY MARTINI: Turu was just a pure Japanese warrior when I met him, five-feet-six, one hundred sixty-five pounds. He was the bodyguard during *The Mike Douglas Show*. Muhammad Ali was downing Sly. He was saying that Sly was a sellout and an Uncle Tom right before the commercial break. Sly goes, "By the way, Muhammad, where do you live?" The audience starts laughing and

Muhammad started freaking out because Sly got in the last word. Ali lived in a big house in a White neighborhood in Cherry Hill, New Jersey. Ali said, "You better watch it—you better get out of Philadelphia." Turu stepped up. Muhammad looked at Turu and backed up.

HAMP "BUBBA" BANKS: He was supposed to have been Bruce Lee's sparring partner. He was Sly's man Friday. Turu was very quiet. I never seen him get into anything. Sly built all these images; Turu was supposed to be the killer.

JERRY MARTINI: Turu saved my ass many a time on the road when I was drunk. The police were coming after me and he intervened. When Rusty Allen was in the band, we were in Buffalo at the Holiday Inn. We were all drunk and the police were harassing Rusty. I took a piece of ice and threw it at the cops and it hit one in the back of the head. They walked over and said that they wanted to talk to me. They wanted to beat the fuck out of me. I'm hanging onto the chair and the cop was grabbing me by my neck, trying to pull me up.

Turu came over—he had a way of doing things—and took the guy's hands off me without any violence. Turu swoops me out of the chair and says, "Let's be careful." Poor Sid Page. He played violin; it was his first night with us. He comes walking up and they grabbed him and threw him in jail for being drunk and disorderly. He didn't know anything. They grabbed him because nobody wanted to fuck with Turu. He was soft-spoken, very quiet, but he had power. He had green eyes. His father had green eyes. His grandfather had green eyes. They were all warriors.

HAMP "BUBBA" BANKS: Black, that was my man. Ken Roberts wound up taking him from me, the most unpredictable motherfucker I had with me. Black and I did shit for Ken Roberts, too. Godfather shit. Ken was mad with somebody over in Little Italy in Beverly Hills, up there where O.J. lived in Brentwood. They had a horse up in Ken's house in Mandeville Canyon. Black and I took the horse down the street. Black drove and I held the horse outside the window. We left the fucking horse in the middle of the street, like a $350,000 racehorse. We just left it there.

STEPHEN PALEY: I had an artist that I was recording and he had a tune that I thought could benefit from Sly's input as a producer. Sly, as a favor, made the track for me. The trouble was, the track came out too well and the kid couldn't sing over it. It was too funky and Sly wound up using it himself on one of his albums. Jimmy Gray Hall was the artist and the song was called "If That's Not Loving You." But then when Sly recorded it, he changed the melody and the words and called it "That's Loving You." To be honest, Jimmy Gray Hall's version was better. The song was better. Sly should have just done it, given him co-credit and not changed it. It had a better melody and better lyrics, but he could never sing believably over the track. It was so sad. I actually got Sly to do something for me as a favor and it turned out too well to be used for my purpose.

TWELVE

NOBODY BELIEVED ANYMORE

Sly, Central Park West apartment, 1973.

KEN ROBERTS: Then he moved to Novato. He wanted to move back up to San Francisco. He was up there for a year or so. He had different problems with the state of California and taxes. He had an accountant named Sidney Frank. Peter Bennett, at the time, came and looked into things; he was a tax attorney originally. He looked into some of these things and saw that these returns weren't accurate. He advised Sly not to sign those and have them redone. He hired another couple of accountants and they redid those. In the meantime, he kept having these problems because he kept spending, spending, spending. Then he lost the house up there. He lost the house because the IRS or the state of California wouldn't settle with him, wouldn't release the lien that they put on him in order for him to refinance it.

RUSTY ALLEN: One time we were up in Novato sitting in the living room. I missed something. The next thing I know, Kathy was sitting on the couch and Sly stood up in front of her, and before Bubba could catch him and stop him, he just slapped the shit out of her. But then there were times that they seemed really happy. He would come home with roses.

KATHLEEN SILVA: I wasn't really happy with that world. It wasn't what I wanted. I was dealing with it because I thought that I couldn't go anywhere. I had started there at such a young age. I always felt hopeless and trapped and I had no money. Things were done for me. Phone calls were made for me. If you want to call it a pedestal, I guess it could be, but in a way it hindered me. It was almost like being captive. It was very frustrating. When I would run away, I didn't know how to get anywhere. I couldn't find my way out of a paper bag. Women who have been abused by a man, either physically, verbally, or whatever, they can't explain why they didn't leave or run away. You feel like you have no strength, that you can't help yourself, that you have to stay because where would you go? What would you do? I've been hit by him before, very badly. I am lucky I survived. I was just sucked into his world and I was going down the drain. It took my child coming into my life. That was something that showed me I didn't need to be on that hill, in that house, or driving a Mercedes in order to survive.

STEPHEN PALEY: The Pit. I've been there. It was very plush. It was a studio where the control room and the studio became one because Sly didn't really do that much live recording. It was all direct into the machine. It was like a carpeted pit. The whole thing was circular. I think he had a bed in there. There was a Jacuzzi and a bedroom—it was a whole suite. It was only for Sly. Chris Stone, the guy who ran the Record Plant in Sausalito, built it for him.

TOM FLYE: He started hanging around with [Record Plant co-owner] Gary Kellgren. It was hard enough to record Sly in a real studio. In a studio that had a studio and a control room, 90 percent of the stuff was recorded in the control room anyhow, even his vocals. He insisted on doing most of them in the control room. It was kind of a problem because he would do his vocal and change the horn parts. He would insist on the vocals being loud, so I would have to go back and spot erase between every word and get rid of all the old horn leakage on the track. It was really a nightmare. There was always leakage with the big speakers. We would waste a lot of time doing technical b.s. work to try and get it back to where it was supposed to be.

The whole thing of the Pit was that it was going to just be a control room with all the instruments in the control room. Luckily, I was able to keep it so we kept the drums in the studio when I worked with Sly. But the horns we did in the control room, all the guitars and basses. We would always move the B-3 organ into the control room, although I was able to keep the Leslie speaker out in some room someplace.

The basic room was about twenty-five by thirty-five feet, maybe, and we dug a hole down into the room. Basically, we sunk a big, cement bathtub into the room because it was at sea level. You dig down and suddenly you got seawater. This is what he had talked about for years. Usually control rooms are built up in the air, just a few inches, so when you are in the control room, you look down into the studio. He kept saying, "I'm tired of looking down into the studio; I want to look up into the studio." For quite a while he would make that comment; I didn't think much of it. But that is kind of what happened. The boards and the tape machines and the keyboards were sunk down into the middle of the room in a pit—that is how it became known as the Pit.

It had a ramp down to it and the back of it was like a big couch. It had pillows and everything. Everybody could just sit around. There was like a drum area on the regular level, off in one corner, and then there was another station where you could put an amplifier, if you wanted an amplifier. It was all one room and there was a token control room glass in front of the board that was like six inches high, like a windshield. There was a bedroom, a bathroom, and a small little lounge, all attached to it. When it was finished, he moved in.

JERRY MARTINI: It was the weirdest room I've ever seen. Downstairs there was a little room with a heart-shaped bed and the studio was built in a pit in the ground. They came up with this weird material like behind an amusement park with fake little rolling hills made out of Astroturf, with wild colors. It was uncomfortable to play there. It was like a dream.

When Ken Roberts took over, he was the person that really took away anything left [of] Sly and the Family Stone. He completely destroyed that. He would say, "If Sly walked out, you guys wouldn't be nothing," Maybe he was right. But there would have been no Sly if wasn't for the whole Family Stone intact, the original band. He was the focal point, but there was so much talent in the original band that it never would have gotten off the ground if he had tried it just as Sly. He wouldn't have got off the ground if it wasn't for me pushing his ass. He was stuck right where he was and he was very happy with being a disc jockey. But Ken Roberts changed the money thing.

So I rehearsed with Santana for three months. I was going to have a side of an album, all my songs, because we were going to do a Latin funk album. I wrote so many songs. My second wife used to write songs. Carlos came over to my house all the time and we would practice my songs. It was a different avenue to go for him. I think it would have been really great. Then he met John McLaughlin, who at that time was Mahavishnu, and Carlos snapped into this other thing. I lost everything on that, all my time invested. So Lynne and I hurried up and wrote this ethereal song so I could at least get one song on the new album, "Borbolleta." We wrote "One With the Sun" for him—"We are in time with the music of the universe." I just threw some chords together. It was nice. I made about forty grand on it.

> From *Associated Press*, November 8, 1974: "Rock music's most sensational marriage, which opened with a Madison Square Garden ceremony before 21,000 guests, is ending discordantly, an attorney revealed yesterday. Sylvester 'Sly' Stewart, 31, leader of the rock group Sly and the Family Stone, is being sued for divorce by his wife of five months, the former Kathy Silva, 21. She contends Sly has stolen their child."

Kathleen Silva with Sly Jr. Novato, 1973.

KATHLEEN SILVA: I tried to go for a divorce and he was trying to reconcile with me. He flew me to Hawaii. They had a job out there and he knew that I would be happy in Hawaii because that was my heritage. He was trying to patch things up. We were in this beautiful suite, and the baby was crawling around in his little diapers, pretty baby, beautiful face. We had reconciled. But that was when I first found out that he had a daughter with somebody in the band, Cynthia, the horn player. I had no idea that she had already been born or anything. I found out on the plane to Hawaii. Sly had fallen asleep leaning on my shoulder. I had to go to the bathroom and I had my little baby in my hands. I got up to go to the bathroom and I bumped into Cynthia—they were in coach, we were in first class.

"I need to talk to you—I have to tell you something—nobody wants me to tell you, but I think you should know," she told me. "I want you to know that Sly and I have a baby girl." I was crushed. I burst into tears. We were trying to reconcile and he never told me this. His mother and father got very upset at her. They said she never should have told. It was a very ugly scene and I thought it was very sad. It also hurt to find out the child's name. "What is her name?" I asked. She says, "Phun." I said, "I guess it was, then, wasn't it? You named it well," and I walked out.

I wish she never told me because that was one of the first spikes that went into my heart and showed me that I could never make this world pretty again. It was just going to get uglier and uglier. It was tearing my heart up.

When we went back to the mainland, the limo at the airport took me to Novato, to the mansion up on the hill, forty-three acres around it. The guy who built the house was the architect who designed all the houses in the town and his house was at the top of this mountain. Six-stall stables for horses with running water—I love horses—peacocks running around once again. It was a beautiful retreat, nice, old-country, woodsy. The driver dropped me and my son off, opened up the front door, and let us in. He was going to the studio with Sly. I hadn't been in the house for almost a month. I was going through the house because it was dirty, nobody had taken care of it. I walked upstairs to put the baby in his room and laid him down for his nap and bottle.

I started to clean way down in the kitchen, the way I usually do, from one end to the other end. I went through the bottom floor of the house and started on the top. My baby must have woken up and heard me up there. He climbed out of his crib—he had just turned two. He was walking towards me, down the walkway. There were chandeliers in the center of this huge entry hall. I opened up my door and there's Gun, wild-eyed, bushy-tailed, and not having eaten for two weeks.

My baby and the dog locked eyes. They were on the same level. And we were in a bloody battle from then on. The dog was an English pit bull with a horse's head and little Japanese eyes. That whole mouth went over my son's head. He started ripping him apart, shaking his head and trying to devour my son. I was screaming and trying to figure out how to get my baby's head out of his mouth without ripping his face all up because of those fangs in his head. I couldn't just yank him away from the dog. I had to get the dog to release his mouth and pit bulls don't do that.

Gun and I were fighting for Sylvester and I had no other thought. I couldn't think anymore. I had no more time and I was exhausted. I grabbed my baby in my stomach like a football and I went down on my knees. I leaned over to get one hand down on the ground to become an animal like him. I stared into his eyes and growled like an animal to frighten him. I became him. It was the only thing I could think of to get him to understand. I became an animal, a mother animal. He immediately stopped and looked at me shocked. I said, 'That's right.'"

I started growling like a vicious animal and I kept on going towards him and he started backing up. The screen door to the balcony was open and he walked out onto the balcony. I slammed that glass door shut and I locked it. I said, "You stay there, you asshole, I'll be back." My legs were like jelly. I was trying to figure out how I was going to get down those stairs without dropping my son. All he was doing was staring at me and he was all ruby red, bloody. I couldn't even see where the cuts were because they were bleeding so badly. I was holding onto him and his ear and I was trying to make it down the circular staircase.

Somehow, I managed to find the keys to my Mercedes. I started running towards the carport—there was like a six-stall carport, too. I jumped in and laid my son across my lap, holding his head. I saw these beautiful white eyes and all this red blood all over. I drove down the hill. I never met my neighbors before and I saw these children playing at this house about halfway down the hill. I drove in and they came up to the door, and then they backed up, frightened because they saw my son. I said, "Where are your parents? Quick, go get them now, hurry." They came running out and I started shaking. "Please help me," I said. "I don't know where the hospital is. My son has been attacked by my dog. I don't know what to do. Please help me. I have to get to the hospital." They took me into their house and they laid him on a pool table and called an ambulance.

That whole white wall on the second-story entry hall was full of my son's blood. He ripped off half of my baby's skin from his left ear. I held it and took it to the hospital. He had over a hundred and twenty stitches from the shoulder up. He was just beginning to talk and he was immediately catatonic for a month and a half. This was the rudest of my awakenings and when I decided that there was no other thought but to leave. That was it. Nobody cared for us. There was no safety involved. There was no way to help my child. All alone, screaming at the top of this hill, forty-three acres around me and nobody to help me, nobody to hear it.

RUSTY ALLEN: He still had some of his religious values somewhere in there. He was fucking up, like we all were. There were some conversations about that where he said, "I think I have done too much shit, too much wrong, and I don't think God will take me back." He didn't say it to me, but he said it to somebody in the group. I think he did take it seriously. I took it seriously.

KEN ROBERTS: From 1971 to 1974, the one concert that he didn't show up at was Washington Capitol Center. That was the last concert that I ever did with Sly. Other than him playing Radio City Music Hall [January 1975] and bombing out, that is the last concert he ever did in his life. We did a whole series of concerts, then we played Capitol Center. I got him back into various cities that didn't want him because they were afraid of him. We played Capitol Center. We did it with Cellar Door Concerts, and he was a big success. Eight months or so later, we decided to do it again with Graham Central Station on the bill.

By that time, he was tied in pretty much with Chris Stone from the Record Plant. I had started to look into the studio charges and things like that. I saw that we were being charged for our studio time while we were on the road. I didn't make a friend of Chris Stone when I stopped that. Chris Stone, at that point, started telling him he should be getting rid of me, that I was a bad influence on him, etc. At various times when Sly would take drugs, he wouldn't be coherent. Never in my entire time with him did I ever see him take any drugs. I saw the results of it. I could see it.

Any newborn baby could see it. I never saw him take it. I never saw any drugs around him. That sounds ridiculous, ludicrous. I used to say dope is for dopes.

There was a gig at St. John's University where the whole thing started with Chris Stone says this, Chris Stone says that. Chris Stone got into this whole thing where Ken is no good, don't listen to him, and this and that. Sly would get easily swayed with whoever he was standing with at that minute. Maybe Chris Stone gave him money, I don't know what he did. I have no idea. At St. Johns, I said to him, "Sly, we only got a couple more to go. Forget about me. I will stay out of the way. The bottom line is, you better be there."

"Memo From Miller" (syndicated newspaper column), December 15, 1974: "Sly and the Family Stone will be remembered for a long time on the campus of St. John's University in New York for a concert he never did perform. Over 3,000 students paid an average of five dollars each to see Sly's campus concert the other weekend for the benefit of both the college and muscular dystrophy. Sly never showed at all for the rehearsals and finally appeared for the first time over an hour after the concert was supposed to have started. He was doing the third number of his act when he just stopped singing, walked offstage, and tried to leave. Sly was unable to make his escape because other cars had his limousine blocked in the parking lot. As concert promoters, who were paying Sly $16,000 for his one performance, converged on the car to try and talk him out of running out on the concert, Sly bolted from the car and ran away. The college promoters chased after him. They all wound up running around the college's football field before Slippery Sly finally was able to make it back to his limo and make a speeding getaway."

RUSTY ALLEN: Him and Ken got into it before the show. Something about they were supposed to be donating money to kids with leukemia or something. For some reason, Sly and Ken were feuding and Ken couldn't get what he wanted. So that was one of those things where the gig got sabotaged. Sly appealed to the whole crowd, said we couldn't do this right now because Ken was holding up his money. Just some strange shit.

KEN ROBERTS: He was in New York City, and we were sort of on the outs. From time to time, he had certain people coming to him and saying get rid of Ken Roberts. We can do this for you. We can do it better. He would go along with their trips but never do it. He would listen to what they had to say. All the people in his family used to see that I was there for him. I was always there for him, no matter what. Along with him came all of them. I made money. But by the same token, that is what I was supposed to do. I wasn't born with him in the hospital. I was doing what I did. The last thing I had anything to do with was Capitol Center. I kept checking. At this particular time, he had an apartment next to mine at 25 Central Park West in New York City. I was in IB and he was in 1C. I really wasn't talking to him at that moment. I told him the day before, "Don't be a fool, this is the last show of this series."

HAMP "BUBBA" BANKS: We were in New York and the plane was waiting on us. Sly was just laying on the bed. I was sitting at the foot of the bed saying that the plane is ready. The band had left already.

KEN ROBERTS: When I went to the airport, they said that he was leaving now. The group had already left. I got to the Washington, D.C., airport, I called the auditorium, and they said he is still in New York. I said, that is it. It is too late now. I got on the plane and went back to New York. He left the group stranded there. Larry Graham went on. I told him if he misses a gig, that is the end of me. He couldn't get me on the telephone again. He tried the next week to talk to me. I wouldn't talk to him. Never spoke to him again.

> From *New York Times*, January 18, 1975: "It is the middle of January and we already have a candidate for 1975's pop-music rip-off of the year—or if not rip-off, then at least bummer. The perpetrator was Sly and the Family Stone, which out of some well of egotism out of touch with recession realities booked itself into the 6,000-seat Radio City Music Hall for eight shows. Thursday night's opener attracted an official count of 1,100 and it looked smaller."

JERRY MARTINI: I was there in the beginning and I was dedicated all the way up to what I consider the end. The Radio City thing clinched it for me. At Radio City, I didn't even have enough money to get home. We started on a DC-3 and ended up on a DC-3. We went from the DC-3 to Elizabeth Taylor's private eleven-seater jet. There was a rise and there was a definite fall. We were barnstorming in Texas at the end. By that point, our self-esteem was very low. I used to have to call and beg for money. We weren't getting paid. The band was disintegrating. They didn't even have any tickets for the band to go home. We had no money. Ken Roberts didn't really like anybody. He liked me better than most of the other guys. He hated Freddie. Freddie gave Ken Roberts a bad time. Freddie, at that point, was a pretty hostile guy. Cocaine drove Freddie crazy. He was subject to be violent. He was real cocky. He hit Ken Roberts. He knocked his glasses off. Freddie was pretty good at kung-fu. He was pretty accurate. He said, "This time I knocked your glasses upside your head—the next time I'm going to knock your head upside your glasses." Ken always treated me better than the other members, besides Sly. Ken secretly paid me and gave me a ticket home.

We were used to playing for 26,000 screaming and yelling people at Madison Square Garden and had dropped to playing Radio City Music Hall for a couple hundred people. That stunk. Shitty rooms at the Mayflower Hotel across from 25 Central Park where Sly lived. No more per diems; they were out the window. The Radio City thing was a fiasco. Nobody came. Kool & the Gang was the opening act and they did better than we did. Only three or four hundred people were there. Nobody believed in him anymore.

PAT RIZZO: That was pretty crazy. Nobody got paid. We had plane tickets to fly home, but no money. Everybody tried to say we're not going on until we get paid. Jerry and I somehow made it to the airport to get out of town. That could have been the last live gig.

HAMP "BUBBA" BANKS: Ken Roberts broke the group up. What happened at Radio City was that we found out the group gets no money. They get two hundred and fifty dollars per show. They come from three or four thousand to two hundred and fifty. Wean me, but push me off the cliff like that and I say, "Rose won't be getting that—we outta here." I took Rose. When Ken came in, it was like five thousand dollars a night. When it went down to two hundred and fifty dollars, I knew Rose and I weren't going to be in it anymore. I just wasn't going to let her prostitute herself like that. It wasn't really about the money, but about the abuse you had to take. I said, "Fuck no—no more of this."

KEN ROBERTS: I wasn't there. He just needed money. He was just getting money. There was no Kapralik. There was no Ken Roberts. It was only Chris Stone. He wasn't getting any money from Chris Stone. He still had his deal with CBS, but he wasn't delivering anything. His only source of income was going to be personal appearances. Chris Stone, I think, set him up with Donjo Medlevine. I think Donjo paid him $100,000. Donjo said that was the worst experience of his whole life, and he had some pretty bad experiences.

CYNTHIA ROBINSON: I did not feel good about that gig. I didn't feel in good form. After a while, not rehearsing took a toll on me, because if we didn't rehearse, I didn't play unless we were on a gig, and that caught up with me. I was busy with my daughter. Not having rehearsals began to take a toll on my playing.

FREDDIE STEWART: All of the sudden, what I was playing was tasteless, empty. I was looking around at everybody else and they were just there. It was sad. I remember looking at a person out in the audience and they were crying. It was almost like they could sense what I was feeling. It was like it was just gone. I was so glad to get off the stage. I was through. Guitar was out of key and I couldn't tell it until forty minutes into the set. Everybody else was sounding bad. No purpose, nothing happened, there was no magic. All of that was gone. All mechanical. No feeling, no emotion. Everything has hit the fan. All of these interrelationships. Everybody was tired. Nobody wanted to do it. Nothing held together.

RUSTY ALLEN: I stayed until something happened. I was in L.A. Sly was up north. I called him collect. The operator said, "Will you take a collect call from Rusty Allen?" "Hell, no," he said and hung up the phone. I was like, "Damn, I was playing with this guy a week ago—how can he cut the umbilical cord that easy?" But it wasn't shit to him.

CYNTHIA ROBINSON: I never quit the band. I just stopped getting calls for gigs.

FREDDIE STEWART: It is sad to say. He knows what he didn't do. He knows what we wish he had done. I know he wishes he could have done better. By me and by a lot of other people. I think he thinks about it all the time.

THANK YOU

Thanks to all the courageous people whose interviews comprise this account of a story that was often painful for them to tell. These people dredged up scenes from something that, in most cases, seemed like a past life to them. They were generous with much more than just their time.

Everyone who granted interviews was enthusiastic and supportive, but Hamp Banks worked diligently at tracking down what he liked to call "the other so-called gangsters," and his endorsement was crucial. David Kapralik also took time to show me his up-country Maui on a day I'll never forget for its beauty and spiritual warmth.

Bradford Gates and Rich Prasch sorted through the long hours of tape-recorded interviews to produce the transcript. Thanks, too, to Lee Hildebrand, who conducted some of the interviews on Sly's early days (Shelby Givens, Tiny Mouton, Johnny Morris, John Turk, Alan Schultz, Mike Stevens, David Froelich).

Thanks to libraries everywhere, but especially my tireless colleagues at the *San Francisco Chronicle* library and the periodical reading room in the main branch of the San Francisco Public Library. And thanks, also, to my employers at the *Chronicle*. Let me single out my editors, Liz Lufkin and Mark Lundgren, who have been particularity supportive of this project.

Thanks to Jayson Wechter Investigations. Also, thanks to Jim Doyle at the Chronicle, Kitsaun King at Santana Management, Ben Fong-Torres at the *Gavin Report*, and Gregg Errico, who helped find important subjects. And thanks, too, to Natalie Neilson, for so much. John Traglia of Casto Travel helped me get there. Cherie Attix at Hale Ho'okipa Inn, Makawao, made hers a home away from home. Thanks, always, to Bob Merlis at Warner Brothers Records. And thanks Lisa Lashley at Sony Music.

Thanks to Daly City Bob Cattaneo for the records; Alec Palao for sharing the research for his excellent CD compilation of Sly's Autumn Records years, *Precious Stone*, on Ace Records; Rico Tee of Rhythm Records; and the late Mark Edmonds of Baytown Records.

Other writers whose previously published work in the field was both inspiring and illuminating include Ben Fong-Torres, John Grissim, George Trow, Peter Hassinger, Cliff Jones, Greil Marcus, Roy Carr, Joe Wood, and Al Aronowitz, among others. David Ritz offered sage counsel.

Thanks to other toilers in the vineyard, like Jon Dakss, who runs a fabulous Sly and the Family Stone fan website; Neal Austinson, Jr., whose video collection and magazine file were treasure troves; and Brian Copeland, who is working on a film with Jerry Martini.

Thanks also to Jules Broussard for the opening sentence.

To Dave Marsh, thank you, my brother. Thanks to Sandra and Harry Choron. And always, thanks to Frank Weimann of Folio Literary Management.

Special thanks to Keta and Carla.

And, of course, Thank You (Falettinme Be Mice Elf Agin).

DISCOGRAPHY

SINGLES

Stewart Four
"On the Battlefield "/ "Walking in Jesus' Name" (Church of God in Christ, Northern California Sunday School Dept. 78-101) 1952

Stewart Brothers
"The Rat" / "Ra Ra Roo" (Ensign 4032) 1959 "Sleep On the Porch" (Keen 2113) 1960

Danny (Sly) Stewart
"A Long Time Alone" / "I'm Just a Fool" (Luke 1008) 1961

Sylvester Stewart
"Help Me With My Broken Heart" / "A Long Time Alone" (G&P 901) 1961

The Biscaynes
"Yellow Moon" / "Uncle Sam Needs You" (VPM 1006; 1961

The Viscaynes
"Yellow Moon" / "Heavenly Angel" (VPM 1006) 1961
"Stop What You Are Doing" / "I Guess I'll Be" (Tropo 101) 1961

Sly Stewart
"I Just Learned How to Swim" / "Scat Swim" (Autumn 3) 1964

Sly
"Buttermilk Pt. 1" / "Buttermilk Pt. 2" (Autumn 14) 1965
"Temptation Walk Pt. 1" / "Temptation Walk Pt. 2" (Autumn 26) 1965
"Sly Stone: Rock Dirge Pt. 1" / "Rock Dirge Pt. 2" (Woodcock 001) 1971

Note: An early demo session by Sly and Freddie Stewart, released at the height of Sly and the Family Stone's success

Sly and the Family Stone
"Underdog" / "I Want To Take You Higher" (Epic 10229) 1967
"Dance to the Music" / "Let Me Hear It From You" (Epic 10256) 1968
"Life" / "M'Lady" (Epic 10353) 1968
"Everyday People" / "Sing a Simple Song" (Epic 10407) 1968
"Stand!" / "I Want To Take You Higher" (Epic 10450) 1969
"Hot Fun in the Summertime" / "Fun" (Epic 10497) 1969
"Thank You (Falettinme Be Mice Elf Agin)" / "Everybody Is a Star" (Epic 10555) 1970
"Family Affair" / "Luv & Haight" (Epic 10805) 1971
* "I Can't Turn You Loose" / "I Ain't Got Nobody (For Real)" (Loadstone 3951) 1971
"Runnin' Away" / "Brave & Strong" (Epic 10829) 1972

"(You Caught Me) Smilin'" / "Luv & Haight" (Epic 10850) 1972

"If You Want Me to Stay" / "Thankful 'N' Thoughtful" (Epic 11017) 1973

"Frisky" / "If It Were Left Up to Me" (Epic 11060) 1973

"Time For Livin'" / "Small Talk" (Epic 11140) 1974

"Loose Booty" / "Can't Strain My Brain" (Epic 50033) 1974

* "Get High On You" / "That's Lovin' You" (Epic 50135) 1975

* "Le Lo Li" / "Who Do You Love?" (Epic 501750) 1975

* "Crossword Puzzle" / "Greed" (Epic 50201) 1976

* "Family Again" / "Nothing Less Than Happiness" (Epic 50331) 1977

* "Remember Who You Are" / "Sheer Energy" (Warner Bros. 49062) 1979

* "The Same Thing (Makes You Laugh, Makes You Cry)" / "Who's To Say" (Warner Bros. 49132) 1980

ALBUMS

Sly and the Family Stone
A Whole New Thing (Epic 24324) 1967
Dance to the Music (Epic 26371) 1968
Life (Epic 26397) 1968
Stand! (Epic 26456) 1969
Greatest Hits (Epic 30325) 1970
There's a Riot Goin' On (Epic 30986) 1971
Fresh (Epic 32134) 1973
Small Talk (Epic 32930) 1974
* *High On You* (Epic 33835) 1975
* *Heard Ya Missed Me, Well I'm Back* (Epic 34348) 1976
* *Back on the Right Track* (Warner Bros. 3303) 1979
* *Ain't But One Way* (Warner Bros. 23700) 1982

COLLECTIONS

Woodstock (Medley: "Dance to the Music" / "Music Lover" / "I Want to Take You

Higher") (Cotillion 500) 1970 The First Great Rock Festivals of the Seventies: Isle of Wight/Atlanta Pop Festival

Note: Sly also appeared on: *Soul Man: Original Motion Picture Soundtrack* (A&M Records) 1986

Jesse Johnson: Shockadelica (A&M Records) 1986

SLY STONE: PRODUCER
SINGLES

Gloria Scott & the Tonettes
"I Taught Him Pt. 1" / "I Taught Him Pt. 2" (Warner Bros. 5413) 1964

Bobby Freeman
"Let's Surf Again" / "Come to Me" (Autumn 1) 1964 "C'mon and Swim Pt. 1" / "C'mon and Swim Pt. 2" (Autumn 2) 1964 "S-W-I-M" / "That Little Old Heartbreaker" (Autumn 5) 1964 "I'll Never Fall in Love Again" / "Friends" (Autumn 9) 1965 "The Duck"/ "Cross My Heart" (Autumn 25) 1965

The Spearmints
"Little One" / "Jo-Ann" (Autumn 7) 1964

Beau Brummels
"Laugh Laugh" / "Still In Love With You Baby" (Autumn 8) 1964 "Just a Little" / "They'll Make You Cry" (Autumn 10)

1965 "You Tell Me Why" / "I Want You" (Autumn 16) 1965 "Don't Talk to Strangers" / "In Good Time" (Autumn 20) 1965

Mojo Men
"Off the Hook" / "Mama's Little Baby" (Autumn 11) 1965 "Dance with Me" / "Loneliest Boy in Town" (Autumn 19) 1965 "She's My Baby"/ "Fire in My Heart" (Autumn 27) 1965

The Vejtables
"I Still Love You" / "Anything" (Autumn 15) 1965

Chosen Few
"Nobody But Me" / "I Think It's Time" (Autumn 17) 1965

Great Society
"Someone to Love" / "Free Advice" (Northbeach 1001) 1966

Little Sister
"You're the One Pt. 1" / "You're the One Pt. 2" (Stone Flower 9000) 1970 "Somebody's Watching You"/ "Stanga" (Stone Flower 9001) 1970

Joe Hicks
"I'm Goin' Home Pt. 1" / "Home Sweet Home Pt. 2" (Scepter 12266) 1969 "Life and Death in G & A Pt. 1" / "Life and Death in G & A Pt. 2" (Stone Flower 9003) 1970

6IX
"I'm Just Like You"/ "Dynamite" (Stone Flower 9002) 1970

ALBUMS

Bobby Freeman
C'mon and S-W-I-M (Autumn 102) 1964

Beau Brummels
Introducing The Beau Brummels (Autumn 103) 1964 Volume 2 (Autumn 104) 1965

MISCELLANY

Billy Preston: *Wildest Organ In Town!* (Capitol 2532) 1966
Note: Contains three Billy Preston-Sly Stone originals, including the original version of "I Want To Take You Higher," mistakenly titled "Advice."

Sly & the Family Stone: "I Can't Turn You Loose"/ "I Ain't Got Nobody" (Loadstone Records 3951)

These were the first demo recordings by Sly and the Family Stone, licensed by studio owner Leo Kulka to Loadstone in lieu of payment for studio time. These two tracks, along with the other two pieces recorded at the same sessions ("Life of Fortune and Fame," "Take My Advice"), have been reissued on a number of different labels.

*Note: The period covered by this book ends with the dissolution of the original Sly and the Family Stone, although Sly continued to make records with some of the same musicians.

Photo Credits

About the Author

Author photo by Deanne Fitzmaurice

Joel Selvin, who covered pop music for the *San Francisco Chronicle* since 1970, remembers where he was when he first heard "Dance to the Music." He has written more than twenty other books about pop music including the number one *New York Times* bestseller "Red: My Uncensored Life in Rock" with Sammy Hagar. His other books include an award-winning biography of Ricky Nelson, a best-selling account of the sixties' San Francisco rock scene, *Summer of Love*, the biography of songwriter Bert Berns, *Here Comes the Night*, and his best-selling investigation, *Altamont; The Inside Story of the Rolling Stones, Hells Angels and Rock's Darkest Day*. He lives in San Francisco's Potrero Hill district.